LATE VICTORIAN NEEDLEWORK

FOR

VICTORIAN HOUSES

a facsimile of
The Lady's Handbook of
Fancy Needlework

AMERICAN LIFE FOUNDATION

WATKINS GLEN, NY

1979

ISBN : 0-89257-048-2

Production notes:
Design and production was undertaken by
Walnut Grove Graphics and Book Production,
Watkins Glen, NY. New composition in
Linotype Caslon was done by Tier Old Style
Typesetting, Binghamton, NY. Printing and binding
was done by Valley Offset, Inc.

The original from which this facsimile was taken
came from the Research Collection of the
American Life Foundation.

RESERVING AND RESTORING a Victorian home is an arduous task. In most cases the house is a skeleton of its former existence. With any luck the former owners did not succumb to the seductive calls of the asbestos and aluminum siding salesmen. But often the gingerbread has been removed in some ill-advised attempt at modernization. The garden and landscape have usually disappeared as well. Inside, the furniture is gone along with some of the ornament; the wallpaper lies under layers of paint.

All this is self-evident and the remedies well known. But what is one to do about the perishable needlework? Any perusal of old photographs of Victorian interiors leaves one with the impression that the needlework was as important as the mouldings, wallpaper, chairs, tables, and cabinets. Victorian houses need Victorian needlework, and this is the book that can help.

Actually, it is four-books-in-one: [1] *Children's Fancy Work*, [2] *The Lady's Lace Book*, [3] *Ornamental Needlework*, and [4] *Macramé Lace*. With one of the biggest building booms of today taking place in the doll house business, many will like the first part, with its needlework for children, their dolls and doll houses. But the book is mostly about needlework for interiors, and that is the chief reason for reprinting it.

For much of the twentieth century it has been fashionable to scoff at Victorian interiors, especially their masses of needlework. But, oddly, there has been a revival of Victorian needlework by the young people who have come to the nineteenth century via the Arts and Crafts Movement. It is typical of them to share their interiors with prodigious amounts of macramé, embroidery, and plants, the result being a kind of neo-Victorian clutter. Many professional interior decorators have also made neo-Victorian clutter fashionable. It also appears to be a practical thing. Caroline Seebohm, in her article in the February, 1979 *House & Garden*, "In Search of a Quieter Life," recommends "Nine ways to cut down the noise levels at home." Number one is "Place furniture, blinds, wall fixtures, lamps, or curtains in a room to break up the standing waves created by parallel walls." And number two is "Use carpet or fabric on walls to help absorb noise, as well as carpet on floors." The Victorians, a historic people who never enjoyed the dubious benefits of snowmobiles, chainsaws, motorcycles, power mowers, and emergency sirens, had the right idea.

Given this kind of support, no longer is there any justification for Victorian house lovers being timid about putting Victorian needlework back into their Victorian interiors.

THE LADY'S HANDBOOK

OF

FANCY NEEDLEWORK.

CONTAINING

FOUR HUNDRED NEW DESIGNS IN ORNAMENTAL NEEDLEWORK, LACE OF SEVERAL KINDS,

INCLUDING GUIPURE, MACRAMÉ, PUNTO TIRATO, ETC.;

AND ALSO

FULL AND PRECISE INSTRUCTIONS FOR THE WORKING
OF EACH DESIGN.

FULLY ILLUSTRATED.

LONDON:

WARD, LOCK, AND CO., WARWICK HOUSE,
SALISBURY SQUARE, E.C.

PREFACE.

—◆◇◆—

THERE are few pleasanter occupations than fancy needle-work, which can be taken up at any moment, and, while em-ploying the fingers, allows the mind the freedom necessary for a train of thought or the conduct of a conversation. The present volume comprises four different sections. The first will be found useful by those who have experienced the difficulty of amusing children, containing, as it does, suggestions for their employment in various light and yet useful ways, which, while affording a kind of training for the fingers, amuse their little owners and keep them out of mischief.

The second part of the book deals with the inexhaustible subject of lace and its home manufacture. The lover of lace-work will find here some beautiful and original designs, together with the clearest possible instructions and suggestions as to the purposes of dress and decoration to which the various patterns may be applied.

The third section includes a wider area. Ornamental needle-work as treated here may be applied to an article as small as a pincushion or one as large as a window-curtain. Care has been taken to give only the newest designs, and to exclude everything that is old-fashioned from the scope of the work.

Macramé lace forms the subject of the fourth and last section. Here we give not only new, beautiful, and thoroughly practical designs, but instructions which comprise every stage of the work, from the buying of the materials to each kind of stitch used in producing the most intricate pattern. It is the first time that clear instructions have been published in company with such a number and variety of lovely designs, and as Macramé lace promises to supersede even crewel-work in popularity, we have little doubt that our efforts to make the manual as complete as possible will find some meed of favour in the eyes of the public.

INDEX.

CHILDREN'S FANCY WORK.

DOLL'S-HOUSE AND FURNITURE.

How a Child may Amuse Itself—Stringing Beads—Card-Work—Dolls'-
Houses—Making—Papering—Furnishing—Furniture made of Cardboard
and Cane—Whatnot—Mirror—Wardrobe—Model Gardens, Farms, &c.

GIRLS, from the tiniest upward, will generally amuse themselves for hours with their dolls; and if they possess a small
pair of scissors (which can be bought for sixpence at any fancy
repository, with *round* and blunt tips, especially intended for
children's use), they can, if mother will supply them with odds
and ends of silk, &c., cut out things, and adorn their dollies as
they please. If, too, they are allowed needle and thread—and
the tiny mites will soon become careful with the former rather
dangerous toy if taught early—they can fashion the pieces into
caps, pinafores, or whatever their fancy dictates, and to have
cut out and made something all their "very own selves" is
infinitely more pleasant to their little feelings than the gifts
from mother or nurse of more elaborate constructions. Stringing beads is another amusement of which girls are generally
fond, and it offers what is most tempting to the child-mind—
variety—as so many things can be made with a few bright-
coloured beads; but care must be taken that baby's rosy mouth
is not made the receptacle for a great number of them, as will
be the case if the chubby fingers are allowed to meddle with
the "pitty sings." With a few pieces of perforated cardboard
dolly can have brooches, lockets, sprays for the hair—in fact,
quite a display of jewels. Some of the grown-up members of

1

the family can cut the cardboard into different shapes—oval or heart-shaped for lockets, round or horseshoe for brooches—and the children, armed with fine needles and thread, can sew on the beads, making different sets of ornaments with the different coloured beads, say a turquoise and pearl with pale blue and dead-white beads, a ruby and diamond set with deep red and sparkling white ones, &c., arranging the beads as they fancy or as mother suggests, and finishing with a setting of yellow or steel beads for gold or silver, as the case may be. Then dolly must have a jewel-case. Any small box with a lid, such as a Tamar Indian box, does beautifully for this; it can be stuffed with wadding and lined with pink or blue silk, under the supervision of some older person (the children, though, doing all the work, for in this will be the pleasure to them); then the necklaces, brooches, &c., are laid in in regular order. Little slits may be cut for the rings, which may be strung on the cotton or worked on narrow strips of the cardboard and button-holed over to make them neat. If the children are not equal to the task of buttonholing, no doubt mother will help.

Endless as is the variety of amusements to be found for the little ones, nothing gives so much real and lasting satisfaction as a doll's-house, and this, like many other things, can be made at home if there happen to be a good-natured big brother who will condescend to interest himself in the work. There are always packing-cases about, stored away in cellar or attic, one of which could be spared for the purpose; this, then, with a few deal boards, some two-inch screws, a pair of hinges, some nails and smaller screws, a hasp for the door, glue-pot, and last, but not least, the willing brother or uncle with his box of carpenter's tools, can be quickly converted into a charming *doll's-house.* The case, after being thoroughly cleaned, should be set on end, and the places for floors and partitions marked out, if only large enough to admit of two rooms, so much easier to make, as it will only want one shelf in the middle for the bedroom floor, the end of the case itself doing duty as a floor for the sitting-room. If large enough to admit of *four* rooms, then a piece of board should be sawn off evenly, the edges, all but the front one, smeared with glue, and this should be fitted into the case, at about the centre; this would be the bedroom floors; then, after proper measurement, another piece of wood should be prepared and slid in edgeways between this floor and the ceiling at about the middle; this will be the partition wall between the two bedrooms; for these should certainly both *be* bedrooms, not allowing one to be used as a drawing-room, for children may thus be taught, even in their play, that it is necessary to health and wellbeing that sleeping accommodation should not be in any way curtailed.

This floor and partition may be made firm by the use of the two-inch screws, which can be driven in from the outside, the heads being concealed by papering when the carpenters have completed their work, and the house is in the hands of the paperhangers. After this, a partition of the same kind will be required below to separate the sitting-room from the kitchen. The papering should be done before the door is put on, as the house is much easier to turn about then. White foolscap does best for the ceilings, and any scraps of wall-paper can be used for the other parts, only care must be taken that the *pattern* on the paper or papers is small, or the rooms will be dwarfed and ugly.

If the wax and china ladies who are to inhabit this little mansion are æsthetic in their tastes, and insist on a dado in their parlour, it can be made thus:—Take some white foolscap, such as that used for the ceilings, cut it to the length required for the walls, then with pencil and rule draw some faint lines on the paper perpendicularly and about an inch and a half apart. This done, cut some strips of coloured paper, blue, green, or red, whichever best suits the tone of the room, and paste these on the white paper (using the pencil lines as a guide), bringing them to within three inches of the bottom ; then add a horizontal line of the same to hide the ends.

1.—DOLL'S WINDOW-CURTAINS.

Now comes the dado, the making of which will give intense

delight and amusement to the little ones. If wanted very simple, turn out mother's collection of crests. pick out the

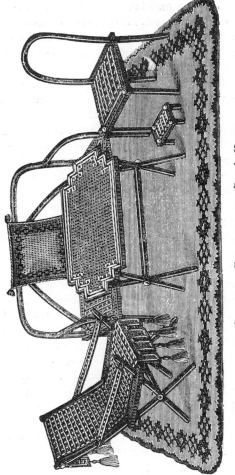

2.—CARDBOARD FURNITURE FOR DOLL'S HOUSE.

darkest, and arrange them as they look best on the white paper you have left below the horizontal strip of coloured. The crests should be stuck on with gum, as it is better for them than paste, and when tastefully arranged they have a pretty effect; but a much more elaborate one can be made thus: collect all the old valentines, Christmas cards, &c., those which you do not particularly care to keep, and pick off or cut out from them all the tiniest figures of birds, insects, &c., with which these works of art generally abound; these, with some bunches of flowers, miniature trees, and tiny cupids disporting themselves in the shade, will, if arranged so that the birds appear to be flying or perching on the branches of the trees, and the insects crawling about beneath among bright flowers and grasses, make quite a charming dado, but it is much more difficult to make than the other, though the planning of the attitudes for the different figures will, as we have before remarked, afford great amusement. In this, too, mother's paint-box will be required, as the foreground will want "touching up" a bit; but with a little patience and perseverance all slight difficulties can be surmounted.

Our paper-hanging being finished the next things to be considered are the carpets for the different rooms. Strips of ordinary carpet of a neutral tint, or with a coloured stripe on a dark ground, will do for each room if such strips are to be found; if not, then they must be manufactured by the children themselves. For pieces of a large-patterned carpet—a geometrical, for instance, or one with sprays of leaves or huge bunches of flowers —would be altogether out of place here. We may be thought "fussy" on this point, but we cannot help thinking that it is bad for the children if the idea is allowed to grow on them that "anything will do," even when they are only, at play-work. *If a thing is worth doing, it is worth doing well.* This is one of the wise old saws which, coming from the lips of their elders, are apt to be thought very tiresome by juveniles, but the practice of which, in early life, has been wont to bring forth good fruit in

6

after-years. So with the furnishing of our doll's-house, though it is only nominally for the *amusement* of the children, there is no reason why it should not have care and attention bestowed upon it when it may, like Miss Edgeworth's tales, combine instruction with the amusement. But to return to our carpets : if no such scraps as those which we have suggested can be found, then they can be made out of old strips of cloth or thick flannel joined together, a bright and a dark stripe alternate; or if the strips are all dark they can be worked over at the seams with coloured wool in chain, feather, or herring-bone stitches. A carpet of this sort will do nicely for the sitting-room. As carpet underneath beds is supposed to be a great error in the sanitary arrangements of a house, we must have small rugs instead, which can be easily made. Little bits of black or white fur, remnants from the children's winter garments, make admirably warm rugs, and look most effective when edged with scalloped cloth or flannels like "real skins." These can, in summer, be superseded by others of a lighter description made out of cloth or rep. The door may now be put on, and to take off the box-like appearance it may be covered with folds of chintz firmly nailed on—unless there be any one among the party clever enough to cut away the wood and insert panels of glass ; in that case the appearance would be much more elaborate, to say nothing of the pleasure for nimble little fingers in making up and arranging curtains to suit the different interiors. When the door is in its place the furnishing proper may begin.

Boxes containing chairs, tables, whole suites, in fact, of every kind of doll furniture, may be bought ranging in prices from one shilling to a pound and upward, as advertisements say; but we want to have as little as possible to do with the toy-merchant, or rather we wish to be our own toy-merchant, so we must look round us to see what can be utilised and pressed into service. And here, if anywhere, we shall find the truth of the Scotch proverb which tells us that *many a mickle makes a muckle,* which being Anglicised means that one never ought to despise small things ; certainly things of the sort we want can be made out of almost nothing. We will begin with our bedrooms—and here

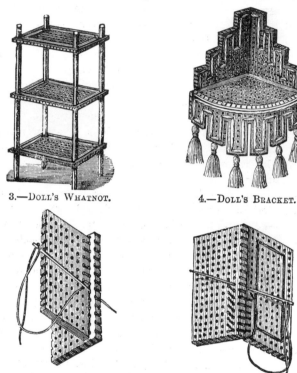

3.—Doll's Whatnot.   4.—Doll's Bracket.

5.—Detail of **7**.   6.—Detail of 7.

our imagination will have **to go a** long way in the matter of a fireplace, for what with beds, washstands, and other necessary furniture, we have no room for a mantelpiece of any description —therefore we advise the ladies who use these rooms to leave their bedroom doors ajar at night, as they cannot have a

" register " to open for ventilation. The larger beds for these rooms can be made out of night-light boxes, using the lid as a

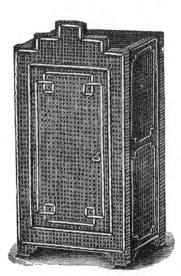

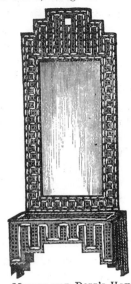

7.—DOLL'S WARDROBE.   8.—MIRROR FOR DOLL'S-HOUSE.

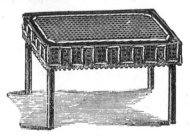

9.—DOLL'S TABLE.

tester, and sewing to it draperies of muslin or silk, or by cutting away the sides of the box, excepting half an inch at each corner (which will serve for the legs), and turning the lid back over the

9

bottom, sewing the two together to keep them firm, we have an orthodox art bedstead without draperies of any kind to harbour dust or other impurities. There will probably be babies in our house who will want bassinettes or smaller beds of some kind. Match-boxes made in the same way as the foregoing will answer this purpose, or for a very tiny—a miniature Tom Thumb— baby a large walnut-shell makes a good cradle. We need not give directions for the making of mattresses and pillows beyond the suggestion that bran is not good for filling these, as it is apt to get full of worms or mites, which will soon destroy them, besides infecting other articles of furniture.

Pretty little blankets overcast in coloured wools, lace-edged pillow-cases, and sheets (with Dolly's monogram perhaps) are, of course, indispensable. Strips of white knitting or crochet joined together in the manner suggested for the sitting-room carpet will make pretty coverlets for these beds. Having finished these beds, we will turn our attention next to the toilet-tables; as these can be covered and draped in every imaginable way, a slight roughness and uncouthness of outline can well be hidden. Before giving directions for making these heavier articles of furniture we would suggest that a collection be made of small boxes, wooden and others, not excepting pill-boxes, which will be useful; also pieces of wood from broken toys, such as the " stand" from a donkey or goat. Out of this heterogeneous mass can be picked a piece or pieces of board for the tops of the dressing-tables. These can be shaped with a pocket-knife, holes bored on the under side for the legs—slips of wood the required length—which should have one end of each pointed and dipped in glue or gum and inserted in the holes.

When the gum is dry and firm the tables may be covered with chintz, or muslin over glazed calico—any way in fact, in which fancy may dictate. We will suppose that some kind friend or relation will present the dolls with looking-glasses; but even the making of these is not a hopeless matter. One we

10

made some time since was a tolerable success. It was a tiny oval glass, which had at some time or other fitted into the lid of a work "companion." It had a twisted gilded wire about it,

10.—Work Case for Doll's-House.

which gave it a finished look; but as it would neither stand nor hang, we made a pedestal for its support out of an end of a lath, such as is used for a window-blind. It was very smooth excepting two ends, and these we rounded with a penknife. With this,

ii

too, we carved a couple of pillars from the same wood, and polished the whole by well rubbing in a little sweet-oil, which also gave a golden-brown tinge. We then drew some black lines and scrolls here and there with a quill pen as a little ornamentation, bored some holes with the points of the scissors, and stuck in the carved pillars, one at each end of the flat piece of wood. The ends of the glass were then well smeared at the back with

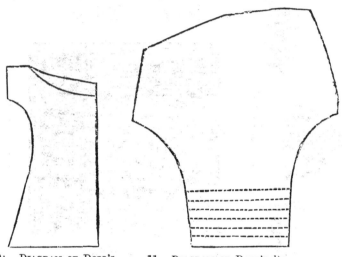

10A.—DIAGRAM OF DOLL'S CHEMISE.　　11.—DIAGRAM OF DOLL'S DRAWERS.

glue—gum was not strong enough for this—and we stuck it against the pillars, having when dry a pretty little looking-glass.

Washstands can be made in much the same way as the dressing-tables, only not being draped they will require more careful workmanship. Some attempt at carving must be gone into for the legs; the slabs can be painted and veined to imitate marble. The necessary accessories in the shape of jugs, basins, soap-trays, &c., must, we fear, be procured at the nearest

12

toy-shop. The only hint on their manufacture we can give is this: the china mouthpiece of a tin trumpet, when plugged at the bottom, makes a capital basin, but jug to match there is not. The making of a wardrobe is very simple: five straight laths, each about an inch and a quarter in breadth, and a few tin tacks

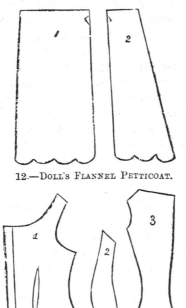

12.—DOLL'S FLANNEL PETTICOAT.

13.—DOLL'S PETTICOAT BODICE.

being the chief necessaries. Two pieces of wood should be an inch and a half longer for the sides. Place these upright and nail in short nails about the eighth of an inch apart from each other, then nail it across the back at the top, turning the tacks inward, these being the pegs for the doll's dresses. Instead of a door, this wardrobe can have a curtain in front, made in this

13

way:—Hem a piece of chintz, and through one end run a drawing string—a piece of piping cord or very narrow ribbon; at each end of the top of the wardrobe place a small gilded nail, and fasten the curtain to these by the drawing string. Chairs are not easy to make, but even these are possible if made in the shape of a folding deck-chair. Two long pieces of wood, with two short ones stuck across, form the back; the same sort of thing answers for the seat, then by placing the long ends crosswise at the bottom, and running a strong nail through, the legs are formed. Pretty little cushions made out of scraps of silk or velvet, and stuffed with wadding, should be placed on these as a finish. Having now finished our bedrooms tolerably, we must begin upon odds and ends for the sitting-room, as we want things a little more elaborate here. The best plan to commence with is to buy a shilling box of plain furniture and upholster them in silk, velvet, or satin; tiny scraps will answer the purpose. A score or two of *very small* brass nails—those about the size of a pin, only shorter—will be wanted, and a little wadding for stuffing. The chairs when bought will probably be painted red or green, with papered seats; but their tints will not matter so very much, as the backs and seats will be entirely covered. To do this, lay a little cushion of wadding on the seat of a chair, then stretch over it the velvet, or whatever is to be used for the coverings; cut the size required, turn the edges in neatly, and fasten it to the chair by means of the brass nails, stuck in carefully and at regular intervals round the edges of the seat. The back can be covered in the same way, first inserting the cushion of wool, and to give a neat appearance when the chairs are turned round, finish the backs by stretching a piece of velvet across and bringing it round to meet the front piece, nailing the two together.

Chairs and sofa having been finished, there comes a question of tables; these will have to be made, as the one tiny monstrosity, if we may be allowed the paradox, which will be found

in the box, is too hopelessly ugly for anything excepting the
kitchen. A five-o'clock gipsy tea-table is easily manufactured,
the round lid of a tooth-powder box answering admirably for
the top ; this can be covered with velvet, and have a valance of
narrow lace or fringe; then three legs must be carved of the
right length and stained black. Indian ink does nicely for this,
or, if a polished stain is required, a little black sealing-wax
dissolved in spirits of wine will give it. These, when dry, can
be stuck into holes bored for them in the top, and the table is
finished. A large table is rather more difficult, but we made
one in the following manner which has done duty for over two
years, and is still perfect : we got a small painted stand with
four wheels, which served as castors ; the stand had once served
as a means of support for a tiny lamb, which had, however, long
since disappeared; in the centre of this we stuck a cork about
two inches in length for the pedestal, and over that we set the
top, which had been the lid of a toy tea-set box—this, with
a velvet cover, made a fitting accompaniment to the rest
of the furniture as a centre table. A tiny square wooden
box, with the lid stuffed and covered with velvet, in the same
way as that described for the chairs, and the sides stained, makes
a good ottoman, while small pill-boxes, *stuffed tightly* and covered,
answer as footstools. A pretty mantelpiece can be made out
of empty cotton reels cut in half lengthwise, the flat sides to be
used for the back; three of these will be sufficient : a Coats'
machine cotton reel for the base, and two smaller on the top of
it, one above the other ; these will be the pedestals, and a long
straight piece of wood stretching across the top will be the
shelf. This can be covered in velvet and fringe, and be the
receptacle for the doll's family china. If the pedestals are formed
of *white* reels there will be great scope for artistic decoration,
as groups of flowers, birds, &c., may be painted on them, or
etched in Indian ink. A small oblong wooden box (white), such
as one sees in the toy-shops, containing frogs, ducks, &c., will

15

make a good chiffonier by standing it on end and slipping in a
piece of wood or stiff cardboard at about the middle, to stand
as a second shelf. The box may then be stained black, and a
trail of leaves painted on the lid, or a suitable picture be
gummed on to imitate a panel; four black beads stuck on, one
at each corner of the top, will give a finished appearance to this
piece of furniture.

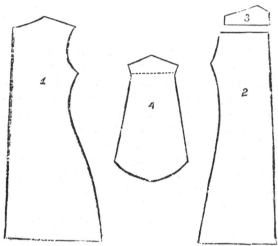

11.—Doll's Nightdress.

For wall-pictures and tiny hand-screens none can be more
effective than those which we have seen made by a lady (who
kindly allows us to describe them here) for her children's doll's-
house. Small square or oblong pieces of stiff paper were cut
and covered with velvet suited to the tone of the different rooms,
the velvet being kept in its place by stitches across the backs.
On these were gummed small pictures cut from a sixpenny sheet
of scraps, the subjects being suited to the size of the rooms,
such as a diminutive kitten playing with a ball, or a Lili-

16

putian horse and rider leaping over a fence. A margin of
velvet was left all round the picture as a frame, a small loop
of cotton added to the back for hanging, and the *tout ensemble*
was charming, The screens were round, cut out of very stiff
cardboard, handles and all, stained black, with coloured crests

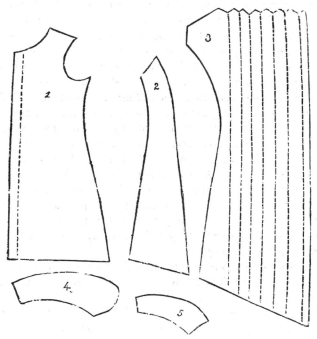

15.—Doll's Dressing-Gown.

or monograms stuck in the centre of each side. These too look
very pretty on the mantel-shelf of the sitting-room.

We now come to the kitchen department, where we shall want
chairs, tables, and a dresser, also a cupboard or two; but as
these will not require such elaborate finishing, we need not give
minute directions on the subject.

The two former can be made in much the same way as described for the bedrooms, without the velvet coverings. Two chairs, with chintz cushions, may be the cook and housemaid's especial property, the others being plain "Windsor." The hints given for the wardrobes will answer equally for the making of the dresser, with the addition of shelves, and without the curtain. Also for cupboards, boxes such as that described for the chiffonier will do. An empty cartridge-case, with a lid cut lengthwise, and a piece of twine fastened round each end as a handle, makes a good candle-box. A square bit of wood will do for a pasteboard, and part of a wooden penholder, with the paint rubbed off, will do for a rolling-pin. Ordinary kitchen utensils, such as tin plates, jugs, and dishes, can be purchased at a penny a box, so that little difficulty will be experienced in filling the dresser-shelves. Gridirons, nutmeg-graters, and frying-pans are also included in some of the boxes. We have not yet attempted to make a kitchener for this room, but we read an account of one some time ago which had been made by a boy out of an old box, so we are tempted to hope that some kind brothers may be willing to help their sisters in this matter also, and with their sharp wits they will probably design something better than we can suggest.

Another simple way of making doll's furniture is as follows: Get some black perforated cardboard and some thin polished cane. For the window-curtains (see No. 1, p. 4) a tiny pole of black cane studded with gilt knobs is required. If the little pole is not ready made, it can be quickly done by pushing the ends of a bit of cane into two gilt beads. The curtains are of white net darned in stripes with white *glacé* thread, and having vandyked edges worked in buttonhole stitch. For the lambrequin, cut two pieces of cardboard in the shape given in the illustration, and sew the two pieces together with long stitches of red filoselle. At the corner of each vandyke are small tassels made of red filoselle. The frame through which the pole passes is of four thicknesses. It is joined to the lambrequin on the side nearest the window. The curtain bands are of twisted or plaited filoselle with tassels of the same. The buckle is a strip of black cardboard stitched with red silk. Two small gilt nails fix the bands to the wall. The blind is of fine white muslin, neatly hemmed at the sides and edged with very narrow lace. The only way to draw this up is by making a wide hem to the top, and putting a thin piece of cane through the hem. This must be set on the top of two nails knocked into each end of the window. It will be very easy to roll or unroll the blind when wished.

No. 2 shows the manner of making chairs, table, and sofa of cardboard. For the sofa the cardboard is of four thicknesses, and of oblong shape. It is then sewn with red filoselle in long stitches, both the length and breadth of the cardboard, forming a checked pattern. Now pierce holes through the four corners with a stiletto, and take a long piece of cane, which must be pushed into the two holes at the back to form the frame. Two more holes are pierced in the back, and through these another piece of cane is pushed and curved. It is fixed to the first piece by a small white stud in the middle. The second piece of cane furnishes the legs. For the front legs and arms two more pieces of cane are pushed through the holes in the front of the seats, and curved to meet the back, to which they are fixed with tiny nails. The cushion is also of cardboard, worked with red filoselle, with tassels of the same. For the easy chair we must make a stand of cane like an American chair. The two front pieces are shorter than the back. The seat and back of the chair are of cardboard, bent to the shape of the illustration with square vandyked edges. They are in one piece, and ornamented, like the seat of the sofa, with red silk. At the corners of the vandykes are small silk tassels. Holes are pierced through the cardboard at the top of the back and where it is bent for the seat part, and the longer pieces of cane are put through them

19

The shorter pieces are then fixed to the front of the chair in the same manner. These two canes are then crossed, and a third piece goes straight between the legs of the chair, and all are

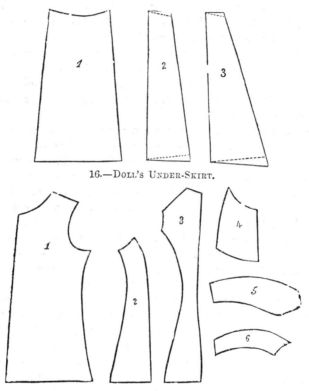

16.—DOLL'S UNDER-SKIRT.

17.--DOLL'S JACKET WITH HOOD.

secured with white studs. The making of the table is very easy: fourfold cardboard cut like illustration and ornamented with long silk stitches. The cane legs are put in in the manner already described, and secured with a stud. For the chair the cardboard is ornamented with the checked pattern of stitches already described. For the back of the chair one piece of cane is used, forming the legs and the curved back. The two front

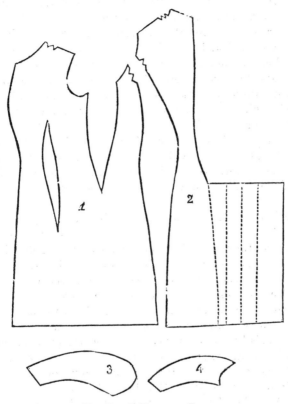

18.—Doll's Princess Dress.

legs are pushed through holes in the cardboard, and headed with a white stud. The footstool is made in the same way. The carpet is of fine red cloth with pinked edge. It is embroidered over canvas in cross-stitch with black silk. When the embroidery is finished the threads are drawn out.

The whatnot shown in No. 3 consists of three cardboard shelves, each four thicknesses, stitched with red silk, and having holes pierced at each corner, through which the canes forming the poles are passed. For the wall-bracket (No. 4) take a double piece of cardboard and bend it in the middle. Then cut the top according to illustration, and work it with red filoselle. The shelf consists of a square piece of cardboard rounded in front and put in corner-wise. It is joined to the back with black silk. The lambrequin is cut in vandykes, and ornamented at each point with red silk tassels.

No. 7. The wardrobe consists of six pieces joined together with black silk. Nos. 5 and 6 show how this is done. The whole is worked with red filoselle, representing panelling. For the hooks, pins can be stuck into the sides and back on the inside.

For the mirror frame in No. 8, double cardboard with the glass glued on to it forms the back. The front is cut out to let the glass show through. This is ornamented with red filoselle in the Grecian key pattern, and joined to the other cardboard which has the glass glued to it with stitches the whole way round. The console attached to the mirror consists of four thicknesses of cardboard. In the middle of the top is a small square hole by which the mirror is hung to the wall.

No. 9. This little table is made of an oblong piece of cardboard of four thicknesses, and with holes pierced at the corners for the fixing of the legs. It has a lambrequin of cardboard, worked in square vandykes with red filoselle.

No. 10. Doll's Work-Case. This is a small cardboard box divided into three compartments, and having a glass lid. It is fitted up with a pair of tiny scissors, a needlecase, and a thimble, mats for the table, &c., and wool of several shades with which to work them. Round the case are several little articles made of cardboard, a card-tray, a folio, waste-paper basket, satchel, curtain-band, trinket-case, date-case, and a needle-book.

Model gardens, lawns, and farms can be constructed easily with suitable materials. Two feet square of stout brown cardboard makes a good foundation for any of these. The remaining materials are dried moss, grasses, glue, sand, small pebbles, a Swiss châlet, box of sheep, cows, farm-buildings, palings, &c. These can all be had at the toy-shop. For a lawn, the foundation must be divided or laid out into grass plots, a hill being added, on the top of which a Swiss châlet is mounted, with garden and drive winding up to it. For grass plats a mixture of dyed and plain dried moss is the best, rubbed small, and put on with glue; the drive and the paths are glued and sanded. The trees, if not included in the box of palings, &c., are best made of dried and dyed fairy or trembling grass or other grasses; these must be set in little blocks to make them stand. A bit of mirror will make a pond or lake, and toy swans put on it. The hill for the house is best made of a block of virgin cork, on which stones and moss are glued.

For a farm the fields are well stocked with sheep and cows, the farming buildings added; carts and straw and haystacks neatly made and fastened on. Skilled fingers can also make fencing on narrow strips of wood of short lengths by fastening wire netting or rustic wood on it. A pretty kind can be made with long strong hairpins, fastened on such closely, and diagonally crossed.

These manufactures will pleasantly employ the fingers of little children during their hours of play, and will not only keep the owners of the fingers out of mischief, but also serve as an educational process for hands and minds, teaching neatness and accuracy, thoughtfulness and ingenuity.

DRESSING DOLLS.

Diagrams for Making Doll's Under-Clothing, Mantles, and Dresses—Doll's Fancy Dresses — Baby - Doll's Dresses — Doll's Trousseau — Walking Dresses—Indoor Dresses—Doll's Mantle, &c.—Dolls Dressed to Illustrate Nursery Rhymes.

WE now come to the most delightful task of all—the making of dolly's under-clothing and dresses. These can be more or

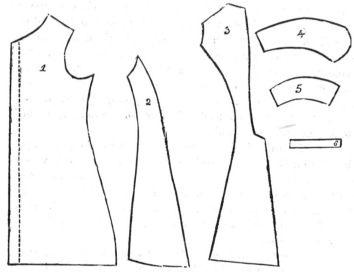

19.—DOLL'S ULSTER OR TRAVELLING CLOAK.

less elaborate according to fancy, but of simple garments the following diagrams will be found excellent models:—No 10A gives a very easily made chemise. It is in two pieces. The diagram gives half of the chemise. The front is cut lower at the neck than the back. It is joined up at the sides with a felled

24

seam ; the bottom is hemmed with a broad hem, and so are the
sleeves. The top is gathered, and set into a narrow band. It
can be made to look very handsome by making narrow tucks in
the bottom, and the sleeves and trimming of lace or narrow embroidery. The top should also be trimmed with embroidery.

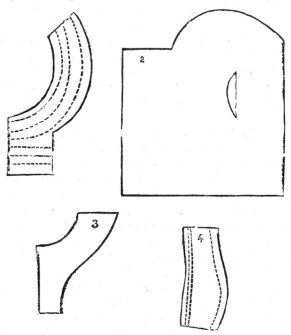

20.—Doll's "Hubbard" Cloak.

No. 11. Diagram for cutting out doll's drawers. This is in
one piece, the band not being given, as it is merely a straight
piece of material. Cambric or percale is nicest for underclothing,
but if the little lady is not possessed of an ample income she
must content herself with longcloth or calico. Two pieces the
shape of the diagram must be cut out. Take one piece and join

the curved parts from top to bottom, in a neat running and felling. Next make the hem at the bottom and above several tiny tucks. The dotted lines show where these should be. A narrow hem must now be made round the upper part, but not along the top. The top is next gathered and stroked ready for setting into the band. Make up the other piece precisely in the same manner and then set both into a band, leaving the deeper part of each leg to the back. The band must be put on carefully and not puckered in the least. A button and buttonhole must then be set and worked on the band, or if this prove difficult, strings of narrow tape can be supplemented. The bottom of the drawers should have a narrow trimming either of lace or embroidery.

No. 12. The flannel petticoat consists of four pieces, but as the back is a perfectly straight piece we do not give the diagram of it, nor of more than one side-piece. For the front take a straight piece of flannel and slope each side very slightly towards the top. The side-gores should be straight on one side and sloped on the other. Join the front-piece and the side-gores together, placing them in the position shown in the diagram, next join the back-piece, which, as before said, is quite plain. The bottom of the petticoat is scalloped and sewn over with Andalusian wool in buttonhole stitch. Where this cannot be accomplished a neat hem, herring-boned on the wrong side, will do very nicely; the middle of the back has a small slit at the top, the edges of which must be turned in and herring-boned. The petticoat is then set into a straight band, all the fulness being drawn to the back and laid in flat pleats. A button and buttonhole or tape strings complete the garment.

No. 13. This bodice is composed of seven pieces of which the diagram shows three, the sleeve being a straight piece sloped slightly under the arm. Cut out the cambric according to the pattern, two pieces of each shape. Next join them together, beginning with a front-piece and one of the side-pieces. The position of the side-piece in the diagram is incorrect; the part which is turned towards the front-piece is really what should be joined to the back. No raw edges must be left in this garment. Every seam must be neatly run and felled. When all are joined a hem must be laid in the top and bottom and neatly sewn. A broad hem is laid down both front-pieces, and on one the buttons are sewn and the buttonholes worked on the right side. The sleeve having been joined beneath the arm and the bottom neatly hemmed is now set into the bodice without any fulness and felled down. The pleats in front of the bodice must not be taken too high. Trim the top of the bodice with embroidery and also the sleeves, and the bodice is complete.

No. 14. For the doll's nightdress take the chosen material, and having doubled it, proceed to cut out the front and back. These must each be in one piece. The yoke and sleeves can be cut out in the same manner with the doubled linen; but as the yoke must be lined, a second piece exactly the same size must be cut out. Now proceed to join the two parts of the nightdress together at the sides, running and felling the seams. The front is slit open a little at the top and tucks run in each side. The back is gathered slightly and set into the yoke. When this is done the front shoulder part is joined to the sloping part of the yoke. A straight band is required for the neck into which the nightdress is set. Trim the opening in front with a narrow band of insertion edged on both sides with a frill of embroidery. Round the neck sew a frill of embroidery and work a buttonhole in the band. Sew a button on the left side. The sleeves must be joined up the whole length and the pointed piece hemmed neatly and trimmed with embroidery. When this is done, turn back the sleeve as far as the dotted lines : this makes the cuff. Now set the sleeve into the nightdress, easing any fulness and bringing it under the arm. The bottom of the nightdress should have a deep hem.

No. 15. Doll's Dressing-Gown. This must be cut in double

stuff, the back not being divided. Join the pieces together in the order of the diagram and lay the back in vertical folds, shown by the dotted lines, or if preferred, gather it in six or

21.—DOLL'S FANCY DRESS.

eight rows at the waist and three or four at the neck. The fronts have a wide hem from top to bottom; buttons down one side, and buttonholes down the other. Set the robe into a small plain collar. Hem the bottom or bind it with narrow braid. The sleeve is plain and tight-fitting. Join up the pieces and hem the wrist, then set it into the robe. The trim-

22.—DOLL'S FANCY DRESS.

ming should be lace or embroidery round the neck and down the front in a shell-pattern; and on the sleeves. Square pockets trimmed with lace can be put on the fronts as a further trimming. The materials suitable for dressing-gowns are coloured flannel, cashmere, batiste, percale, sateen, and muslin.

No. 16. Doll's Under-Skirt. This pattern serves also for a dress-skirt, that being cut out in precisely the same manner. The diagram gives the front and two side gores. The back is a straight piece. Four gores are required, a front and a back piece, making six in all. The diagram shows how the top and bottom of the skirt must be sloped by the dotted lines. The petticoat should be of white lawn or cambric trimmed with flounces of embroidery or with tucks. A broad hem must be laid at the bottom. The back has a slit down the middle neatly hemmed on both sides. The petticoat is set into a plain band, all fulness being drawn to the back.

No. 17. Doll's Jacket with Hood. The half of this jacket is shown in the diagram. Every piece must be cut double, making eleven in all (the hood must be in one piece). Make up the jacket by joining up the two back-pieces. Next join the side-pieces, taking care that the side least sloped comes next the back. Then join the fronts to the side-pieces, and the back and front together on the shoulder. The collar will be a small stand-up band round the neck; this is put on after the hood has been fixed to the back. The jacket need not be lined unless it is of velvet, in which case it should be neatly done with thin silk. If the jacket be cloth, bind the edges with braid, if of silk trim it with fringe, having hemmed the bottom and the fronts. The hood should be doubled and sewn up from the middle to the edge. It should be lined with some contrasting material. When finished it is tacked on to the back so that the point falls in the middle; the collar is then sewn neatly on. The sleeves are plain and tight-fitting, neatly bound at the wrists, and trimmed with a small cuff edged either with fringe or braid.

No. 18. Doll's Princess Dress. This is in four pieces, two fronts and two back-pieces. The side-piece is included in the front. Having cut out the pattern and lining for the bodice part, proceed to make it up by joining the fronts and sides together. Then join the sides and back-pieces together. The shoulder-pieces must now be joined together, and the pleats laid in the fronts. The back-pieces are joined together as far as the skirt. The skirt-pieces are then joined up the middle, and the fulness laid in a broad threefold box-pleat, the top edge being turned in to make it look neat. The fronts are then joined up as far as the bottom of the pleat, and hemmed on each side of the remainder. Here hooks and eyes or buttons and button-holes are set to fasten the dress. If liked the dress can be fastened at the back, the fronts being joined to the top, and the back left open, each side being neatly hemmed and furnished with buttons and buttonholes. A small straight collar is set round the top of the dress. The sleeves are now joined together, the edges bound and then set into the dress. A little further on we give several illustrations of dresses made up and suggestions as to what materials and colours should be used. These should be consulted before beginning to cut out anything.

No. 19. Doll's Ulster. Cut out of double material six pieces like Figs. 1, 2, and 3. Join the two back pieces together to the waist, then allow the left piece to over-lap the left and finish to the bottom of the cloak. This ulster will certainly look much handsomer if it is machine-stitched instead of handsewn. We therefore advise our little friends to coax mamma to do it for them. Having joined the back-pieces together, join the sides and fronts, and then join the back and front pieces together on the shoulder. The front has a deep hem in which the button-holes are worked. The bottom should be turned in and ornamented with six rows of stitching. Round the neck is a small plain collar. A hood like that in No. 17 can be added if liked. The sleeves are plain, having small stitched cuffs. Fig. 6 shows a plain strap to be fixed on the waist at the back with two buttons.

Making these garments for dolly will be an excellent preparation for future usefulness on the part of the small fingers employed. From a completed dress of the dimensions suited to the figure of the largest doll it is an easy transition for the girl,

23.—DOLL'S WALKING COSTUME.

growing out of childhood, to cut out and make some useful article of clothing for herself.

No. 20. Doll's "Hubbard" Cloak. This cloak has a gathered yoke which must be cut out the shape of Fig. 1. Fig. 3 gives the shape of the lining for the yoke. The dotted lines on Fig. 1

show where the gatherings should be. For the cloak, cut out two pieces of the shape of Fig. 2, or if the material is wide enough cut the cloak in one piece. Then join up the back (which is the

24.—Doll's Summer Costume.

shorter part of Fig. 2). The yoke should be cut in one piece if possible, out of double material; so also the lining. Gather the yoke as shown in the diagram and fix it to the lining. Take care in the gathering to turn in the top edge of the yoke far

enough to run the thread of the gathering through both thicknesses. This will form a pretty frill round the neck. When the
yoke is fixed on the lining join it to the cloak, carefully managing
the fulness. The bottom of the cloak should be turned in neatly
and trimmed with lace; the front must be similarly treated, and
hooks and eyes put on underneath so as to be out of sight. The
sleeve (Fig. 4.) is gathered twice at the bottom and once at the
top. The two edges are joined together and it is set into the
slit in the cloak.

Peasant Costumes for a Doll. No. 21. The skirt is of plain
red cambric, with two bands of pale yellow round it, edged top
and bottom with narrow gold braid. White lawn under-bodice
with wide sleeves. The bodice is pleated in front and edged
with narrow embroidery and feather-stitching. Over this white
bodice is a half-bodice of black velvet. The sleeves are tied at
intervals on the arm with two bows of narrow red ribbon. White
lawn apron edged with torchon lace and an insertion of the same.
This apron has *bretelles* passing over the shoulders which are
laced up in front half-way by means of tiny buttons and gold
cord. The bretelles and the skirt of the apron are feather-stitched
with red marking cotton. Pleat the front of the apron into a
narrow band, and set the bretelles on to this. The cap is of
black velvet with a ruche of red ribbon and long streamers of pale
yellow and red. In front of the cap is a small gold-embroidered
design. Round the neck a small gold chain. Red and white
striped stockings and little black shoes with red bows. The
baby-doll's dress is of fine white muslin, the front being trimmed
with tiny lace flounces and muslin frills. This is framed with
lace, which is continued round the bottom of the skirt. The lace
is headed by a narrow strip of embroidered muslin, through the
holes of which a very narrow blue ribbon is inserted. Round the
waist is a pale blue sash tied on the right side.

No. 22. Skirt of Dark Blue Merino, trimmed with two rows of
blue ribbon. Bodice with wide sleeves of fine muslin edged with

lace. Half-bodice of blue merino edged with gold braid and laced up the front with gold silk and small gilt buttons. White muslin apron edged with lace. Conical-shaped muslin cap with streaming ends trimmed with lace and blue ribbon. Baby-doll's-dress of fine white muslin, with deep collar edged with narrow lace. White straw hat, trimmed with pink ribbon. Pink ribbon sash.

No. 23. Walking Costume for a Doll. Skirt, tunic, and jacket of fawn-coloured beige, trimmed with coffee lace and brown satin ribbon. Brown straw hat, trimmed with brown satin ribbon and yellow roses. Veil of yellow tulle.

No. 24. Doll's Summer Costume of Green Sateen. The skirt has three flounces of green sateen, separated by two of very pale pink sateen. The top flounce is headed by two narrow bands of pink. The tunic is trimmed in the same manner as the skirt, but with fewer flounces. Low, short-sleeved bodice with three flounces round the top and the sleeves. The bottom of the bodice is piped with pink and is laced up the back with pink cord. Girdle of pink satin ribbon, to which a small fan is attached. In one hand the doll holds a tiny hand-bag of green silk, covered with pink silk netting. White straw hat, trimmed with pale pink ribbon and a bunch of apple-blossom. Pink stockings and high black boots.

No. 25. Doll's Visiting Dress of Pearl-Grey Cashmere. Half-trained skirt trimmed with puffings and flounces of cashmere, headed by two rows of violet velvet. Tunic trimmed like the skirt. Plain jacket bodice, trimmed with velvet. Black velvet bonnet, lined with pale pink satin. Trimming of pink roses and pink ribbon.

No. 26. Doll in Christening Robe. Cushion of white cambric, trimmed with frills of the same and lace and bows of white satin ribbon. The doll is dressed in a robe of fine muslin edged with lace. White tulle cap, trimmed with a ruche and white veil.

No. 27. Miss Lily's dress is a princess robe of pink sateen with a deep white lace flounce. The jacket is dark red sateen with deep basques and collar of Irish guipure. Small cuffs of the same. The jacket is fastened only at the top beneath a tiny bow of pink ribbon. Each side is ornamented with handsome fancy

25.—Doll's Visiting Dress.

buttons. The front of the dress is pierced by two gold pins connected by a tiny chain. Hat of dark red felt with pink feather and a red bird. Pink ribbon-strings tied beneath the chin.

No. 28. Little Miss Arabella's robe is of soft red silk and white embroidered muslin. The top of the dress is cut square, is piped with red silk, and has a small stand-up frill of fine white crêpe lisse; below are two embroidered flounces, and a third flounce forms the sleeves. The front of the dress has strips of embroidered insertion applied on the silk, the latter showing through the holes. The bottom of the dress is a pleated silk flounce topped by one of embroidered muslin. Broad sash of striped red and white silk tied in a large bow on the left; red

26.—DOLL IN CHRISTENING ROBE.

shoulder-knots. Large white felt hat with a long red feather and a red and white bird on the brim.

No. 29. Doll's School Dress of Brown Percale, trimmed with white lace. The skirt has a deep flounce, which is arranged in two puffings by means of three rows of brown satin ribbon. The top and bottom of the flounce are bound with ribbon. The tunic is divided in front, trimmed with ribbon and edged with lace. At the back, where it is rather long, it is arranged in a puff. The top of the bodice has a puffing of percale edged with lace. Puffed short sleeves. Small brown straw hat, trimmed with lace and ribbon.

No. 30. Carriage Dress for a Doll in Heliotrope Silk. Skirt, tunic, and bodice trimmed with flounces, crossbands, and puffings of silk. Down the front of the tunic are bows of the same. Bonnet of heliotrope silk, trimmed with bows of ribbon and small pansies.

Nos. 31 and 32. Front and Back Views of Doll's Princess Dress, with simulated Jacket of dark blue serge with puffings and flounces of the same material. The jacket is simulated by means of a narrow cross-band of pale blue ribbon sewn round the dress. The neck is cut away square and filled in with frills of narrow lace. Bows of pale blue ribbon at the top and bottom of the jacket and sash of the same at the back. Elbow sleeves with frill and band of serge and edgings of lace. The bottom of the dress has a flounce of white lace. Dark blue velvet bonnet, trimmed with pale-blue bows.

No. 33. Doll's Princess Dress of Black Velvet, with a plastron of the same, edged with red buttons and imitation button-holes of red silk. The plastron is faced with a trimming of red silk, cut bias and ravelled. This also edges the skirt. Small pockets, half of velvet, half of silk. The top of the dress and the sleeves are edged with white lace. Red shoulder-knots. Fancy straw hat, trimmed with red ribbon. Black boots laced with red cord.

No. 34. Doll's Travelling Trunk and Trousseau. The making of the trunk will perhaps prove rather a difficult matter; we therefore advise the buying of it, unless some good big brother or uncle will kindly try his hand at it. But the stocking of the trunk comes altogether into our own particular domain, and can be varied at pleasure. The diagrams already described will serve as models for cutting out the various articles of under-linen and over-wear. Our model possesses half-a-dozen pairs of drawers, six chemises, four nightdresses, six petticoat-bodices, four under-skirts, four flannel petticoats, three prettily-trimmed aprons, three dresses, a hat and a cloak. Each half-dozen articles is neatly tied with blue ribbon and packed in the box. Two of the dresses and the cloak are laid against the lid, and dolly herself wears the third dress standing by the trunk. This is of dark red satin, trimmed with white lace and pale pink ribbon. The first dress in the lid of the trunk consists of a skirt of green cambric, trimmed with flounces of the same edged with lace. The jacket is plain, having double frills of lace on the sleeves and one round the neck. Down the front are bows of narrow green ribbon. The cloak is of tartan, lined with thin black silk. The hood is lined with the same and has a bow of black silk ribbon. Dress No. 3 is of primrose sateen, with a flounce round the bottom and another which simulates a tunic. Each flounce has a heading of black velvet. The belt is bound with the same, and so are the sleeves, and then edged with écru lace. Round the neck and down the front of the bodice is a trimming of lace and velvet ribbon.

No. 35. Costume for a Boy-Doll in Grey Japanese Silk, consisting of blouse with pleated skirt and short trousers. The blouse is piped with red silk and buttoned down the front with large red buttons. Round cap of grey silk piped with red. Broad turn-down collar and cuffs.

No. 36. Costume for a Girl-Doll. Princess dress of pink Japanese silk, buttoned diagonally and edged with narrow white lace. Béret of the same material with a bow of pink ribbon at the back.

No. 37. Doll in Crocheted Costume. Princess dress, hat and boots of pink and white eis wool. A well-fitting pattern must be cut, and the dress begun from the back along 14 stitches according to our model. The pattern is crocheted with a double thread in Victoria stitch, increasing and decreasing as required. The border at the lower edge of the back is crocheted in alternate pattern rows of pink and white wool, the rows crocheted with

27.—MISS LILY.

28.—Miss Arabella.

white wool having the stitches taken out of the back vertical
parts of the stitches instead of the front vertical parts, so that
the pink rows stand out beyond them. Round the neck is a
single pattern row crocheted with white wool. The stitches at
the back breadths of the bodice in those rows which are crocheted with pink wool are taken out of the vertical stitches at the
back, so that the white rows stand out beyond them. The sleeves
are crocheted along 14 stitches. Two pattern rows with pink
and one with white wool; the white wool is continued along
the narrow ends of the sleeve. Lastly crochet a row of double
crochet in the vertical stitches at the back of the previous
pattern row. Then sew the different parts together, and
put in the sleeve, as shown in the illustration. Round the
lower edge of the skirt crochet a row as follows : 1 double in
2nd marginal stitch, 1 purl of 3 chain, and 1 double, repeat.
The dress is then trimmed from the shoulder-seams down the
front, and along the top of the flounce at the back, with 2 rows
of chain stitches of white wool, having 1 pattern row of the dress
between them. To crochet these rows of trimming, pass the
needle from below, upward through the stitch, drawing the
white wool through,* take the needle out of the loop, pass it
through the next stitch in the same way, and draw up this and
the preceding stitches together, repeat from*. Between these 2
rows work slanting stitches, so as to form a vandyked pattern
In front are raised spots to imitate buttons. A row of slip
stitches is worked round the neck, and the dress is fastened at
the back with buttons and loops. The hat is begun in the
middle by closing 3 stitches into a circle and crocheting twelve
rounds, always working in two parts of the stitches, and taking
care to keep the work flat. Then crochet the 13th and 14th
rounds withoutincrease,with pink and white wool respectively, and
turn them back like a revers. The trimming consists of a rosette
made with loops of chain-stitches crocheted with white wool, and
having in the centre a pink ball. The hat is fastened with a

narrow pink ribbon tied under the chin. The boot is begun from the toe with 3 stitches of pink wool, in Victoria stitch. The 1st stitch is missed, so that the 2nd pattern row has 2 stitches. In the 2 following rows increase 1 stitch on the side nearest the instep, and in the 12th, 13th, and 14th rows decrease 1 at the same place. Then sew the narrow edges together as far as the first 4 and last 4 rows of the slanting side for the instep, and the first 7 and last 7 rows of the straight side for the sole, and the stitches at the point for the toe. Round the upper part of the boot crochet with white wool, 1 double, 1 chain, repeat. 2nd row, like the preceding. 3rd row, like the row of purls round the lower edge of the dress.

No. 38. Doll in Bathing Dress. Costume of dark red serge, trimmed with white lace. Waistband of blue ribbon worked in point russe with red silk and tied at the back. Bows of similar ribbon on the shoulders. Bathing cap and sponge bag of oilskin, bound with blue braid.

No. 39. German Doll in Christening Dress. The model stood 9 inches high without the head, and wore a robe of fine lawn, embroidered in satin and overcast stitch and trimmed with red ribbon. The cushion in which it is carried is made of long-cloth, with puffings and rows of muslin insertion over red ribbon. Round the outer edge is a closely-pleated frill of embroidered muslin, and bows of red satin ribbon are sewn down the front. Bonnet of white muslin, trimmed with lace insertion and narrow red ribbon.

No. 40. Doll in Walking Dress. Skirt of black velvet, plain in front and pleated at the back. Round the lower edge a close pleating of cardinal satin. High waistcoat of the satin, trimmed with lace round the neck and fastened down the front with buttons. Jacket of black velvet with turned-down collar and long sleeves bound with satin. The jacket is cut at the neck and waist to show the waistcoat, and is fastened in front with bows of satin ribbon.

No. 41. Baby-Doll. Robe of pale blue cashmere, with short puffed sleeves and close pleatings of the same material. The bodice is cut in a long vandyke which is filled up with pleatings

29.—SCHOOL DRESS FOR DOLLS.

of blue satin and edged with narrow white lace. Similar lace is sewn round the sleeves and cashmere pleatings. Bows and loops of satin ribbon and a blue passementerie ornament complete the trimming.

No. 42. Doll in Evening Dress. Trained skirt of violet corded silk with pleated flounce of satin of the same shade. Above the

30.—DOLL'S CARRIAGE DRESS.

satin is a flounce of white lace, headed by a box-pleating of corded silk piped with satin. Tunic of corded silk, trimmed with lace, and raised in front with rosette and ends of satin

45

ribbon. Short-sleeved bodice of the silk, piped with satin. Collar and sleeve trimmings of white lace and pleated violet satin. Écharpe of satin ribbon at the back.

No. 43. This and the following costumes are exceedingly pretty little dresses, and if enlarged would do for children of two to four years. Master Jack's dress is of white piqué and embroidery. It is of princess shape, fastened at the throat with a single button. The fronts then slope away, showing a plastron of narrow tucks in the middle with embroidery at each side. On each side is a deep piqué pocket. The dress is lengthened by a deep lace flounce. Double turned-down collar finished with a bow of pale blue ribbon. At the bottom of the plastron is a large pale blue ribbon bow. Loose sleeves edged with embroidery. White plush hat turned up on the left side. Above the brim a pale blue silk pompon.

No. 44. Miss Florence is attired in a robe of lace and lace insertion. At the bottom of the dress is a flounce of pleated navy blue silk, above which are three of lace. Plastron of gathered blue silk, framed by bretelles of insertion and lace. Broad sash of blue silk tied on the left side. Elbow sleeves with lace flounces, tied with blue ribbon; white thread mittens.

No. 45. Master Bob's dress is a princess robe of pale blue foulard, having two lace flounces at the edge. The jacket of the same material is trimmed with silk cord. It is fastened with only one button and then falls apart. Deep pelerine collar edged with cord. Round the neck is a frill of crêpe lisse. The sleeves have a small cuff edged with cord and ornamented with a small bow of pale blue ribbon with gold droppers. A larger bow with similar droppers hides the junction of the collar.

No. 46. Miss Lottie's dress is of white batiste with the front cut crosswise, and arranged in narrow tucks. The front is trimmed with embroidery and bows of deep red satin ribbon.

The dress is fastened at the back with buttons and buttonholes, and is trimmed in a similar manner to the front, with the exception of the ribbon bows. The edge of the robe is trimmed with two embroidered flounces, and above is a white batiste sash finished with embroidery in front. Round the top of the dress is a frill of embroidery, and the little sleeves are of the same.

No. 47. Master Harry wears a dress of fine white cambric and embroidery. The back and front are gathered at the top and surmounted by a shaped top of Madeira-work, which is further ornamented with lace. The lower edge has two flounces of embroidery. The junction of the flounce and the robe is concealed by a scarf of shaded red satin knotted in front and tied in a bow at the back. Shoulder-knots of narrow shaded ribbon.

No. 48. Doll's Princess Dress of bright Blue Velvet, fastened aslant and trimmed with flat pearl buttons. Narrow bands of gold braid and a row of guipure lace complete the trimming. At the back, écharpe of blue grosgrain. Short sleeves with shoulder-knots of blue ribbon. Blue velvet hat, raised in front and trimmed with blue ribbon.

No. 49. Doll's Princess Dress with simulated jacket of ivory silk fastened down the centre with pearl buttons and trimmed with crêpe lisse, embroidered with dark red silk. Shoulder-knots and écharpe of dark red grosgrain. Bonnet of soft fancy straw, with bands and strings of red velvet.

No. 50. Doll's Walking or Afternoon Dress of Red Cashmere and Satin. At the bottom is a deep cashmere flounce, which is joined on the wrong side to the over-dress. This is of princess shape, and fastened with hooks and eyes on the right side. Down the front is a gathered waistcoat of red satin. This forms a flounce at the bottom, the edge being trimmed with white lace. A scarf of vari-coloured striped satin is joined to the cashmere fronts. It is laid in four folds. At the sides it is inserted between the seams and passes under the side-pieces, coming out again at the back side-pieces, and again disappearing at the

31.—DOLL'S DRESS.

back. Coat sleeve with cuff of cashmere, into which a small stripe of fancy satin is inserted. Deep gathered collar edged with lace.

No, 51. Doll's Fashionable Mantle. This little mantle is of almond-coloured tricot, stitched with silk of the same shade.

The back is gauged for five rows at the waist, and also gauged a little lower down. The fronts are plain, and buttoned down the middle with horn buttons. Coat sleeve with plain cuff.

32.—DOLL'S DRESS.

Small Mother Hubbard cape set into a plain collar. An écharpe of shaded brown silk is tied in a bow at the back.

Most delightful of all manners of dressing dolls is that of making them illustrations of popular fairy tales or nursery rhymes. This work calls, of course, for more than ordinary care,

49

and because it is so much more difficult, as well as more interesting, than merely dressing dolls in imitation of children or grown-up people of our own times, it should be carefully protected from the dust by being slipped into a box kept specially for it, whenever it is not being exhibited. Dolls dressed in this manner always command large sales at bazaars, or, if merely exhibited at a charge of a few pence per head, will make a decided addition to the funds.

The story of "Little Red Ridinghood" is familiar to all, and not many will need instruction as to what the little dolly who is to represent her should wear. First prepare the wood through which Red Ridinghood must pass. On a square of brown cardboard, covered with thick gum, sprinkle dried moss and grass rubbed small in the hands, sand, and small pebbles. This forms the sward. Now glue one or two pieces of rough cork to represent rocks, and a few trees from a toy village; or make them of trembling grass set in cork trunks. Behind one of the largest trees glue the wolf (which must be bought for the purpose). For Red Ridinghood take a wax or wooden doll, and dress it in a dark blue dress and circular red cloak, with a little hood drawn on to the head. On one arm put a tiny wicker basket, covered with a white cloth. The doll must be glued firmly to the cardboard, half turned away from the wolf.

For "Little Miss Muffet" we prepare another piece of cardboard in the same manner, but with fewer trees (two will be enough). These must be from a toy-box, as our home-made grass trees will not be strong enough for the purpose. The trees should be placed near one end, and stretched between them a cobweb, made of netting or thick white tulle. In the middle is a piece of virgin cork, with tufts of dried moss glued on. Between this and the trees a large black spider, apparently moving towards the rock on which sits Miss Muffet, attired in a dress of primrose sateen, edged with narrow lace, and holding a plate on her knees. A Dutch doll will be best, as the doll should be in a crouching, frightened posture.

Another piece of cardboard thickly covered with moss represents the scene in which the story of " Little Boy Blue" is to be enacted. It is divided into three partitions by means of fencing, which can be easily made, if none is at hand, by soaking dried peas in water until they are soft, and then, having prepared a number of matches by cutting off the heads and pointing the ends with a sharp penknife, pierce the peas with the sticks laid horizontally and perpendicularly. Some of the matches must be cut into shorter lengths than the others. These form the perpendicular posts. A more lasting fence can be made by substituting square bits of cork for the peas, but as cork is apt to blunt the knife very much the peas may be preferred. The moss or grass in one partition should be first dyed yellow with a little saffron dissolved in boiling water, to represent corn, and then glued on to the cardboard. A toy cow is glued among the corn. In the middle partition are a few small neatly-made haycocks, and at the foot of one lies our hero, dressed in blue linen, short trousers, blouse with belt, and a round blue hat lying beside him. In one hand is a small tin horn or trumpet. In the third field, which represents a meadow, the grass may be partly dyed and partly plain dried moss ; the colour can be yellow and red. This will do for poppies and buttercups, but not much of the coloured grass must be introduced or the effect will be spoiled. Here half-a-dozen sheep must be glued, and the scene is complete.

In the story of "Bluebeard" we have splendid scope for dramatic representation. The story may be divided into three scenes. First we have the departure of Bluebeard, leaving Fatima in possession of the key of the fatal chamber. Bluebeard should be a dark-complexioned, fierce-looking doll, with an enormous bright blue beard. He is dressed in Eastern costume, wide green trousers trimmed with narrow gold braid, a white muslin waistcoat fully pleated, and a crimson jacket, also trimmed with gold braid and open in front. Round the waist a gold-coloured sash, and a crimson turban on the head. A curved dagger is stuck into the sash. He is holding out a key to Fatima almost

33.—DOLL'S DRESS.

as big as herself. Fatima wears the dress of a Turkish lady. Long trousers of white muslin reaching the ankles. A skirt of pale blue satin, and bodice of white satin with crimson flowers. The wide hanging sleeves are lined with pale pink. Pink turban and sash of the same colour. Muslin chemisette.

The second scene discovers Fatima standing with hands

raised in horror at the sight of six headless dolls lying at her
feet. She has entered the closed room. Her dress here is of

34.—DOLL'S TRAVELLING TRUNK AND TROUSSEAU.

maize and brown. Maize silk trousers, brown velvet skirt and
bodice, the sleeves lined with maize.

In the third scene Fatima and Sister Anne are seen with
flowing hair, the one wringing her hands, the other looking to

53

the end of the board, on which two tin horsemen are glued. Bluebeard is approaching Fatima with uplifted dagger. His dress consists of purple trousers, yellow jacket, and black sash and turban. Fatima is in white silk trousers, rose-coloured

35.—BOY-DOLL.

bodice lined with white, blue sash and turban. Sister Anne wears peacock blue trousers and bodice, with écru sash and turban.

Little Bopeep, on a moss-strewn piece of cardboard, is surrounded by a flock of tailless sheep. She is dressed in a quilted blue petticoat, a cream-coloured overskirt looped up, with low bodice. Folds of fine muslin are laid round the neck, and fastened in front. On her head is a large-brimmed straw hat, ornamented with tiny flowers. In one hand a crook, with a bow of ribbon and knot of flowers at the top.

36.—Girl-Doll.

"Where are you going, my pretty maid?" makes another capital illustration. The maiden is dressed in a quilted red petticoat, with pale blue overskirt. Over the bodice is a white muslin handkerchief, pinned in front. She wears also a white muslin bib apron. On her arm she carries a milking-pail, and in the other hand a three-legged stool. On her feet are tiny black shoes. Her companion wears a long stiff plum-coloured coat, a scarlet satin waistcoat, white frilled shirt and ruffles at the wrist, white stockings, and black shoes with large buckles. His hair is long and tied with a black ribbon. In one hand he carries a stick, in the other his three-cornered plum-coloured silk hat. The ground on which they stand should be prepared as has been already described.

In the story of " Cinderella" there is room for a great display of talent. In the first scene Cinderella, in a dusty, tattered grey dress, sits barefooted among the ashes of a large fire. The fire-place should be of the old style, with large chimney. A bare floor either of wood or cardboard, with a small brush and dust-pan lying near Cinderella. She is seated on a three-legged stool, with loose flowing flaxen hair falling around her, looking into the fire. Near her is the fairy godmother, a small doll dressed in a short scarlet petticoat, black satin overdress, white muslin neckerchief. A tall pointed black hat, black shoes, and a crutched stick in her hand complete her costume. In the second scene Cinderella is dressed for the ball in glistening white satin. A trained skirt, with overdress of tulle looped up with tiny bouquets of forget-me-nots. She is stepping into the coach, which can either be bought or made. If the latter, stiff card-board will be best for it. It must be elaborately gilded, and open, after the style of a state carriage. The footmen must be dressed in scarlet coats, yellow plush smallclothes, and white stockings. In scene three we have the ballroom. This should have the floor covered tightly with alternate strips of red and white calico. Around the edges of the cardboard settees, otto-mans, and couches must be glued, on which several dolls in gay ball toilettes are seated, with gentlemen in doublets and hose standing or sitting by them. In the middle is the prince, dressed in blue velvet doublet, slashed with white satin, and blue silk hose. He is holding Cinderella by the hand. In a conspicuous place sit the two step-sisters, gorgeously dressed, but with as disagreeable faces as it is possible to procure. The next scene presents Cinderella seated in her old dress, with her foot outstretched. Before her kneels the prince with a small slipper in his hand. The sisters stand in the background, and at each side are the heralds.

The famous story of " Jack and Jill" will not be found difficult of representation. Two scenes will tell the tale. In the first a

37.—DOLL IN CROCHET DRESS.   38.—DOLL IN BATHING COSTUME

green meadow (moss or cardboard) with a cork hill covered with bits of moss, pebbles, &c., and our hero and heroine going up holding an empty pail between them. Jill wears a pink sateen dress and a white muslin apron. On her head a pink sateen granny bonnet. Jack has a striped blue and white suit, consisting of trousers to the knee and full blouse jacket. A round hat on his head, white stockings, and black shoes. In the second scene the actors and place are the same, but Jack has fallen full length down the hill, and Jill is just falling. The pail has rolled halfway down.

The celebrated "Old Woman who Lived in a Shoe" is another favourite. A large shoe of cloth, velvet, or satin, either black or red, is nailed to a board. It is then filled with dolls of both sexes dressed as children. The old woman herself, in a brown dress, white apron, neckerchief, and cap, holds a small birch in one hand, while with the other she retains a little boy-doll, to whom she is going to administer a correction.

CHRISTMAS AND OTHER PRESENTS.

Needle-Books—Toys made from Walnut-Shells—Pocket-Companions—Braces—
Rugs and Mats—Christmas Cards for Nursery Walls—Trinket-Boxes.

ALTHOUGH the knicknacks at the different shops which come
under the head of Christmas presents are so numerous and
varied, and many of them so inexpensive that it might seem
superfluous to make them at home, yet the pleasure to children
of planning, cutting, and arranging little odds and ends is so
great that it is a pity if they are not encouraged in their little
efforts. Some children have such deft fingers that nothing
comes amiss to them; given a pattern they will manipulate their
odds and ends so cleverly that they will soon produce an exact
imitation. Others have not the imitative faculty; they can
originate, but they cannot create; the fingers refuse to work out
what the brain suggests. Others again—and these are the
autocrats—can both originate and create; they have the ready
brain, the quick eye, and the deft fingers; everything they see
starts a new idea. These last are invaluable in the manufacture
of little articles at home. If work flags for lack of material hard
to get, they can suggest a substitute, and not only suggest, but
work it up so that it answers the purpose for which it was required admirably. Still, without the last-named clever one of
the family (as he or she would probably be termed), and with
only moderately sensible heads and hands, the making of presents
at home may go on briskly. There is generally something which
even a "trot" of four may do. Two little friends of ours, one
four, the other seven, made last year (with a very little help
from an older person) a pretty needle-book " for mamma's

59

Christmas present." Besides the pleasure of "working for mamma," the possession of a pleasant *secret* was so delightful to their little minds that for the space of three whole days there was not a single tiny squabble in their domain, much to the satisfaction of every one.

The needle-book was made thus :—Two heart-shaped pieces were cut from the lid of an old cardboard box ; each piece was covered with velvet, the edges being secured by stitches on the inside, not sewn through the card but drawn across from edge to edge. On this was laid a little cushion of wadding for stuffing, this being again covered with a lining of white silk, cut to the shape of the card, the edges turned in, and the whole worked round in coral silk with coarse buttonhole silk. Four scalloped-edged leaves of flannel were added for the needles, two ends of narrow ribbon were sewn at the points of the *heart* as a fastening, and the whole was confined at the other end by similar ribbon, made into bows and sewn firmly on. As the silk and velvet were scraps lying by in the house, the only outlay in money for this little present was about threepence for ribbon and tailor's silk. In making these the form can be varied according to fancy. We have seen one made in the shape of a pair of bellows, secured at the nozzle by a silver thimble instead of strings. As it can be covered and lined with any bright scraps of silk and velvet, or what would be still more effective, with *crash* or *oatmeal cloth,* having the recipient's initials embroidered in silk or crewels, it would with the thimble be a charming addition to a lady's workbasket. If presents are wanted to hang on a Christmas-tree, *size* is not so much an object as *colour;* indeed, for a small tree small articles are best, being lighter, but they must be effective. Dainty little pincushions and thimble-case can be made out of walnut-shells. Scrape the inside of the shell till quite smooth, then stuff a little bag of some bright-coloured material with wadding, making it as nearly as possible the shape of the shell ; sew to this a handle—a bit of narrow cap-wire, covered, answers the purpose—then drop a little liquid gum into the bottom of the shell and press in the cushion. This can be supplied with a pedestal in the following way:—Take two walnut-shells and pierce a couple of holes in the centre of each (a red-hot iron meat-skewer or a knitting-needle will do this beautifully). Now

39.—DOLL IN CHRISTENING DRESS.

place the shells against each other with the holes touching each other, and tie them together with string or fix them with wire. In the upper half the cushion is placed ; the lower forms the stand. For an emery cushion take two halves of a walnut-shell and having scraped the inside, brush over the outside with copal varnish. In both halves make narrow slits in the middle of the sides. Fill a little coloured silk bag with emery-powder and

61

gum it into one half of the shell. Then join both halves of the shell together by means of a ribbon threaded through the slits in one side, and tied in a bow on the outside. Through the openings on the other side draw another piece of ribbon six inches long. This serves to open and close the walnut. A thimble-case is easily made of one half of a shell lined with pink wool stuck on with gum, then inclosed in a tiny bag of its own shape, but large enough to admit of being drawn closely over the opening with a running cord.

Toys made from walnut-shells will please the little ones, and the making of them prove no less enticing.

We give some illustrations which show what can be done in this way. No. 52 is a miniature basket furnished with a cardboard handle. Half a shell is scraped clean and brushed over with gum on the inside, but not too thickly. Then press a piece of coloured silk neatly into the shell, and turn in the rough edges at the top. The piece of silk should be of an oval shape and large enough to just cover the inside. Sew a lambrequin of scalloped brown cardboard round the outside of the basket. The stitches are taken through the silk lining. The lambrequin is worked with pale blue silk before it is sewn to the basket. The handle is also of brown cardboard worked with blue. It is joined on to the lambrequin, the place being hidden by a tiny bow of blue ribbon.

No. 53. This little *bonbonnière* is made of two shells fitting each other exactly. The insides are scraped and then lined with silver paper stuck on with gum. Two holes are drilled in each shell, and through them crimson purse silk is threaded. To this on one side a bow of crimson ribbon is sewn, and on the other two long ends, leaving a loop, are then also tied in a bow. The inside is filled with tiny sweets.

Nos. 54 and 55. These two illustrations show a pretty little toy, the "Surprise" Basket, closed and open. Two exactly-fitting halves of a walnut-shell are scraped clean and lined with pink or silver paper. Holes should be carefully drilled all the way round in both shells, and then a frill of narrow lace sewn round each for the outside and round the inside of the lower one. This is effected by putting the needle through the holes. The edges are then bound with pale blue silk so put on that the stitches do not show. In the lower half of the shell is a tiny wax or china doll with a tiny quilted covering over it. In the upper shell dolly's tiny wardrobe is packed. The shell is closed by means of pale blue ribbon, a loop and end being sewn to each half. On the opposite side is a bow of ribbon.

No. 56. This gives a novel and pretty little purse very easily made with a little help from mamma. Take a well-shaped half-shell and pierce holes round the edge. Then sew a green silk ribbon round it, and to the ribbon sew a little netted bag of green purse silk. Round the bottom of the bag sew four little silk tassels, and through the top thread some twisted silk to draw up the purse. Finish off the ends with little tassels.

No. 57. This is a delightful little toy, and such a pretty addition to dolly's *ménage*. Six holes are drilled into the half of a walnut-shell, and through them coloured filoselle is threaded and drawn together at the bottom, where it is finished with a large silk tassel. Round this tassel six smaller are sewn. Now take a hazel-nut and pierce six holes through it. The upper part of the six strands of filoselle already spoken of is drawn through this nut and tied in a knot at the top. A bundle of coloured filoselle is sewn on to this knot, and in the middle of the bundle is a loop by which to hang the lamp. At each of the holes in the hazel-nut is a tiny tassel of coloured filoselle.

Nos. 58 and 60. Needlebook. Cut the needlebook out of silver *jardinière* canvas according to No. 58. It must then be lined with crimson silk and the canvas worked with crimson silk and chenille after the pattern given in No. 60. Round the inner and outer edges of the canvas sew a narrow fancy braid and make a handle of the same, twisting the braid at the top like Illustration 60. Fill the inside with white flannel leaves with vandyked edges. No. 59 gives another needlebook, also cut out of silver canvas. This is in the shape

40.—DOLL IN WALKING COSTUME.

of a satchel. Cut two pieces of canvas exactly the same size and shape, and embroider each with bright green filoselle in point russe. A feathery star in the centre and two lines following the scalloped outline form the design. The canvas is edged with gold soutache. At the top of the book is a green ribbon, with bows at each end and in the middle. The canvas

41.—BABY-DOLL.

is lined with green silk, not divided at the top. White flannel leaves serve to hold the needles.

No. 61. An Easter Egg. This pretty *bonbonnière* is made of cardboard opening lengthways. It is covered with pale blue silk, and the lower half with finely-braided straw. Round the opening sew pale blue gimp, and furnish the egg with blue silk cord by which to hang it up. The fixing of cord is hidden by two small straw stars. The eggs can be bought in cardboard, and only require ornamenting.

A pocket-companion is most useful when travelling, and is easy to make. A piece of silk, four inches in breadth by twelve in length, should be lined with flannel of the same size, the two being joined at the edges by overcasting in coarse silk or binding with narrow ribbon. One end of this should be round, the other square. The square end should form a sort of pocket, by turning up an inch, and sewing in at each end a round piece of cardboard (a piece cut from a visiting card would be thick enough) covered with silk to match. This pocket would be for reels of silk or cotton. Above this should be two leaves of flannel for needles and pins; again above those should be sewn a piece of elastic about an inch and a half in length, and sewn down in the centre, thus making two compartments, one to hold a small pair of scissors, the other a thimble. The whole can then be rolled up, beginning with the cotton end; the rounded end should overlap, and the fastening be either a button and buttonhole or a ribbon tied round it. A case of this sort, only on a much larger scale, makes a good receptacle for a gentleman's white ties; the ends of the pocket here should be of stiff cardboard, the flannel leaves should be well supplied with stout pins, and instead of elastic for scissors and thimble, as in the lady's companion, this should have two or three small pockets made by stitching across from side to side a piece of flannel about two inches in depth, and dividing it by more stitchings lengthwise. These little pockets serve for studs, sleeve-links, &c., and save a great deal of time which might otherwise be spent in hunting for these small articles, which so often get mislaid.

Another most useful present for a gentleman is a glove and handkerchief case combined. A pretty way of making one of these is to get two pieces of firm, white, and perfectly clean cardboard, each piece to be ten inches in length by seven in breadth; ornament these on one side with narrow ribbon in any bright colour, put on in vandykes, each point to be fastened down with a bead or tiny pearl button. In order to fasten the two cards together they should be laid side by side on a table, and the vandykes be stretched across over the edges nearest each other, thus forming hinges to the back. In the centre of one side should be the word gloves or *gants;* on the other, handkerchiefs or *mouchoirs;* these can have their letters painted in a colour to match or contrast well with the ribbon, or else be cut out of coloured paper and pasted on. The inside should have two pockets made of a lattice-work of narrow ribbon, fastened at the crossings by beads or buttons, the bottoms and sides being secured in the same way to the outside; then to hide the stitches and give a finish to the whole, the edges can be bound with ribbon. A couple of ribbon-strings sewn on at the top and bottom of each side will be for the fastenings when closed. The advantage of the *lattice* pockets is that they will " give" so as to hold a fair number of *gants et mouchoirs.* They should be put in like the pockets in a cigar-case—viz., the bottom of one lying against the top of another, so that when full and closed the case appears of a uniform thickness, not bulging in one place and flat in another; the top of each pocket should be about three-quarters of an inch below the edge of the case.

A pair of braces is always acceptable to a gentleman, and they are easy to make. A strip of white satin jean, cut the required breadth and length (a pattern brace should be got to cut from), will do for the foundation of each brace: on this may be stitched with a machine, or what is more effective, worked on in feather stitch with coarse buttonhole silk, strips of coloured braid—*red* wears best. This braid may be put on in straight lines, a broad line in the centre and a narrow at each side, or a pattern might be traced on the jean, and then worked over with

42.—Doll in Evening Dress.

the narrow braid ; but it must be borne in mind that strength and durability are the great requisites for these articles, and that a raised pattern would probably be uncomfortable. When the outside strips are finished they should be lined with another piece of jean, same breadth and length, and the two (lining and

outside) be bound together by braid. A lining of flannel to
match in colour is most effective, but it gets rubbed into holes

43.—" MASTER JACK."

after a few weeks' wear, and makes the whole look ragged and
untidy.

Proper fittings for these braces can be bought very cheaply, and give more satisfaction than buttonholes worked at each end. Pretty antimacassars, which would give a bright appearance to the nursery or schoolroom, can be made by knitting (in plain stitch) strips about a yard and a quarter in length of coarse white cotton; take three of these strips and plait them loosely together, then sew to this plaited strip one of bright wool, crimson or scarlet, continue these alternate strips till of the required width, and finish off at the ends with tassels of wool. Warm and inexpensive rugs or mats may be made by collecting all the thick rags of the household, light and dark, and cutting them into pieces about half an inch or thereabouts in width; the length is not of so much consequence. These little bits should be drawn with a coarse bone crochet-needle through the meshes of a piece of coarse canvas, such as packing bags are made of, leaving loops to stand up on the right side; if drawn firmly through no fastening is required, and the pattern can be made to suit the taste or fancy of the makers. If light rags predominate, then the centre may be of a light shade and the border variegated; or, if the colours are equal, it might be worked in lines with a border of one colour. This last article, though of course too large for hanging on a tree, is not at all difficult in the making, and with a little practice might well be entrusted to young hands; but to return to smaller articles, more suited to the capabilities of children, penwipers are certainly most simple in construction. The ordinary ones, rounds of cloth scalloped at the edges, all have the figure of a dog, a cat, or a mouse stuck in the centre as an ornament. These figures can be bought for a few pence, and stuck on; but, if this is not liked, the monogram or initials of the person for whom the trifle is intended may be worked with coloured beads in the centre, or cut out in coloured cloth, and sewn on. Tiny wicker baskets, such as can be bought for a penny, look very effective when covered with tinfoil, which can be pressed on with the fingers. These, filled with chocolate-drops or sugar-plums, will be highly appreciated by small friends of the family. The small round baskets used by fruiterers make pretty hand or work baskets when ornamented with ribbon drawn through the meshes, and tied here and there in bows, or worked up into rosettes, a ruching of silk may be added at the top, and a handle made of broad cap-wire covered with silk may surmount the whole. Children always have a lot of Christmas cards lying about, some of them real works of art, too pretty to throw aside, and all of them brilliant in colouring, therefore dear to the children's eyes. These can be utilised in a variety of ways. Pasted on white cardboard, and framed with a plaiting of brown paper, they make pretty pictures for the nursery walls, or pasted side by side on a long strip of brown paper, leaving a tiny margin between each for the fold, they make a novel scrap-book, as they open out in a continuous line; or, again, little frames for each may be made by cutting pieces of cardboard the required size, sewing them together at the ends, and sticking to them with glue bits of cork, or, if procurable, acorns or beech-nuts. A novel way of using broken wine-glasses is to cut a piece of cardboard into a round about four inches in diameter; on this stick pieces of cork—the more rough, jagged, and uneven the better—piling them up a little in the form of a rockery, put in little bits of dried grass and moss here and there, together with a tiny artificial flower, such as a violet, to heighten the deception, and in the centre of all this stick the wine-glass, which should have a tolerably long stem remaining to it. These little things can be used for the toilet-table to hold trinkets, filled with water for a small bouquet, or, stuffed with wool, and the top of the glass covered with a little cap of soft silk or muslin, they make dainty pincushions. Some years ago a workbox or basket was thought incomplete without a piece of wax for thread; such a thing is scarcely met with now, yet it is a most useful trifle, and might be acceptable still to some old-fashioned folks. Little bits of

44.—Miss Florence.

72

45.—MASTER BOB.

wax candle, about an inch in length, answer the purpose; they should have bits of coloured paper cut into vandykes, and fastened round the edges (which should be quite smooth), then another tiny vandyked band turning inward, and a plain one in the centre of the two as a finish.

46.--Miss Lottie.

If a collection of sand and shells has been made during summer visits to the seaside, it may be used for ornamenting small boxes. First cover a box with strong gum, then while it is wet lay the shells on in patterns, and sprinkle sand between them; when dry they are very pretty. If children have a taste

74

for botanising they should certainly be encouraged, as it helps them to discover new beauties in every country walk. Flowers gathered and pressed between leaves of blotting-paper afford amusement for winter days in the mounting and arranging in groups on white paper or card. Autumn again, though bring-

47.—MASTER HARRY.

ing forth more sombre-hued flowers, is rich in its wealth of exquisitely-tinted leaves, brightened for the time by the frost which is helping them to decay. These leaves, gathered before they begin to shrivel, and pressed in the same way as the flowers, can be mounted in all sorts of ways, and if varnished over with hard white spirit varnish they retain their delicate tints for years. Oak and blackberry leaves are among the most

75

lovely of these autumn treasures; they are almost as brilliant as a summer sunset, and, what is a great advantage, they will bear handling, and may be used for screens, covers of blotting-

48.—DOLL'S PRINCESS DRESS.

books, picture-frames, or prettily grouped with tiny ferns and bits of moss intermingled with them, they make pictures in themselves worthy a place in any room.

A pretty little housewife can easily be made of a small doll.

She must be attired in a bright-coloured dress and wear a large
white apron with two pockets, each containing a packet of needles.
The apron should have *bretelles* passing over the shoulders, and

49.—DOLL'S PRINCESS DRESS.

these at the back should have buttonholes worked in them.
Through these buttonholes a bodkin should be thrust having a
reel of cotton on each end.   On the head a small wadded silk
cushion should be glued to serve as a pincushion.

A basket for holding dried flowers, grasses, &c., can be readily made out of odds and ends of cambric, sateen, silk, &c. Four pieces of cardboard, narrowed at the bottom, are sewn together and then covered with any fancy material. The handle is a straight piece of cardboard similarly covered. Over the handle and round the top of the basket is a wreath of rosettes made of ribbon or tape of a corresponding colour to the cover of the basket.

No. 62. Doll's Bonnet of Buckram, covered with rows of black lace and strings of the same, with a rose on the right side; bird of paradise on the brim.

No. 63. Doll's Collar of Pleated Spotted Net, with a bunch of flowers on the left shoulder.

No. 64. Round Steeple-Crowned Hat of White Buckram, covered with white lace. On the left a feather aigrette and wreath of roses.

No. 65. Doll's Straw Hat, trimmed with pink silk and wreaths of roses.

No. 66. Small White Straw Bonnet with White Lace Strings. In front a large bouquet of daisies.

No. 67. Mantilla of Black Lace, drawn together with a cluster of crimson buds.

No. 68. Doll's Collar of Narrow Embroidery and Insertion, finished with a bow of navy-blue ribbon.

No. 69. Doll's Cambric Pinafore with pleated front. It has an embroidered top, waistband, and sleeves.

No. 70. Doll's Brown Straw Hat, with three brown feathers and a brown silk pompon.

No. 71. Doll's Kid Shoe, with straps on the instep.

No. 72. Doll's Cloth Walking Boot, with kid galoche.

No. 73. Doll's Black Glazed Kid Shoe.

No. 74. Fawn-coloured Cloth Coat for a Boy-Doll, trimmed with brown velvet revers, cuffs, and belt.

No. 75. Doll's Black Silk Mantle, trimmed with ruchings, ribbon, and lace.

No. 76. Doll's Brown Cloth Jacket, with gold broché trimming.

No. 77. Sealskin Hat for a Doll, with two brown feathers and a bow of flowered crimson silk.

No. 78. White Straw Hat, trimmed with white feathers.

PAPER FOLDING AND PLAITING.

Paper Windmill—Double Boat—Paper Box—Paper Plaiting—Articles made
from Plaited Paper.

VERY pretty little toys can be made from folded paper, a
windmill being one of the simplest. It is made thus: Take a

50.—DOLL'S WALKING DRESS.

perfectly square piece of paper, and taking two opposite corners
of it, fold one completely over the other, so as to form one
large triangle. Next, open the paper and fold the other two
corners in a similar manner. When the paper is opened there
will be two lines or creases crossing each other diagonally.
With a pair of scissors, or a penknife, slit the paper from each
of the four corners along the fold up to about an inch from the

centre; get a small piece of stick and a pin; take each *alternate* corner and fold it over to the centre; then pass the pin through the centre (thus fastening all parts together), and finally stick the pin vertically into the end of the stick. When held horizontally in the hand of a person moving, the windmill will revolve freely.

To make a double boat fold the corners into the centre *once only*, take each corner in succession and fold it back until the point touches the outer edge of the square. At this stage the

51.—DOLL'S FASHIONABLE MANTLE.

paper is still a perfect square outside, with a smaller square within it. Take one *side* (not a corner) and fold it over to the middle; do the same with the opposite side, taking care that the edges touch evenly in the middle; the folded paper will now be in an oblong form. Turn it over on the table, fold it in half, but at right angles to the previous fold, thus forming a small square; fold one flap downwards towards yourself till the edges meet, turn the paper over on the table and do the same with flap now uppermost. Loosely laid on the table the paper will now resemble the letter W. Hold the W by *the base*, pull out the two folds which are in the first downstroke of the letter (first the right and then the left). This produces one boat; treat the other side in the same manner; this will give the double boat.

To make a paper box. This is made from the preceding double boat (which must, therefore, be made as above). From this point proceed as follows: Take the right-hand boat and pull completely out the point or corner of the paper which is inside, holding the body of the boat firmly all the time between the finger and thumb of the left hand, fold this point down again, outwards, till it is level with the top of the original boat. Then fold the two ends (which formed the bow and the stern) back and outwards, so that the three points touch (outside) in the middle. You have now a square of which you fold down the upper half (outwards). Repeat these operations with the other boat. It will then stand on two of the folds if placed on the table, and there will be two flaps or ledges projecting one on each side. A little management in opening this will now form an open box.

Paper folding can be used for many pretty and useful objects. For the nursery it will supply many little articles to please the eye and ornament the walls. Coloured paper for this purpose can be bought at any fancy shop, and when the colours are tastefully combined they form charming combinations. Nos. 79 and 80 illustrate one of the many forms they may be employed in. Spills of this coloured paper for lighting gas or candles, or papa's pipe, look very well in little boxes made of plaited paper, which process we shall now describe.

A sheet of white or coloured paper is cut lengthwise into narrow strips throughout the entire surface, except a margin of about half-an-inch all round. This is necessary to keep the

strips in place. Some narrow loose strips of paper of a contrasting colour to the first paper are then prepared of the same
width as the strips of the first paper. A wooden needle, like
that shown in No. 84, is also required. This, as the illustration
shows, is a very simple affair, being only a thin skewer of wood
with a notch at one end, into which the strip of paper is slipped.
Having "threaded the needle," proceed to weave the pattern by
inserting the point at the first slit and bringing the needle
through. Now pass the needle through the next slit and the
one following, raising the strip on the needle, just as in darning
one thread is taken on the needle and another left under.
Proceed in this way to the end. For the next row begin with
the *second* slit instead of the first, and continue to the end.
The third row is like the first. Fill up the paper in this
manner to the bottom, and then, turning it to the wrong side,
brush the margin round with thin gum and fix the strips down
on it. If the ends of the strips protrude beyond the margin
they must be cut off. No. 82 shows this design completed,
No. 81 the paper ready for the insertion of the strips. In
No. 83 we have another pretty design, which differs slightly
from the first in occasionally taking up *two* strips at once and
leaving *two* down. When in the middle the design is worked
backwards, copying the first part in reversed position. Innu-
merable combinations can be easily made by simply raising or
lowering a strip at various intervals.

Now a word as to the manner in which these paper plaitings
may be utilised. They can be made into a variety of useful
articles, such as mats, spill-boxes, blotting-cases, card-baskets,
sachets, &c. Mats are made by pasting or sewing the plaiting
on stout paper or thin cardboard, then sew or gum a paper
fringe or frill all round. Strips of tissue-paper, folded and
made into a plait of three, can be substituted for the fringe.
Ruched ribbon will also answer the purpose.

Spill-boxes are made of cardboard, the plaiting being pasted on. They are of cylindrical shape with a circular bottom. The top is ornamented with a *ruche.*

Blotting-books are also made of thin cardboard, with the

52.—Walnut-Shell Basket.

53.—Bonbonnière.

54.—"Surprise" Basket (Closed).

design either pasted or sewn on. The edges are then bound with coloured or gold paper. The sides are next connected by being gummed, glued, or sewn to a strip of tape, and this, when dry, is covered with paper or kid (pasted or sewn on).

55.—"Surprise" Basket (Open.)

56.—Walnut-Shell Purse.   57.—Doll's Lamp.

Sheets of blotting-paper are then fastened on with a piece of elastic or sewn on to the tape forming the back.

Card-Baskets. The frame must be neatly cut out in thin cardboard. The plaited paper is pasted, gummed, or sewn on to each piece of cardboard forming the basket. The edges are then bound with paper or ribbon, and the pieces sewn together or tied with bows of ribbon.

Sachets for pocket-handkerchiefs or gloves. Paste or sew two pieces of plaited paper on to cartridge-paper or thin cardboard. Cut some pieces of silk rather larger than the paper design, fold the silk over the edge of the cardboard, covering it completely inside and overlapping about half-an-inch on the ornamental (plaited paper) side. A silk ruche is tacked or gummed on all round, hiding the overlapping edge of the silk Silk strings are sewn on to fasten the two sides together.

" TWO DOLLS AND A HOUSE OF CARDS."

THIS is going to be such a nice story; it is all about Weddings. There were two new Dollies brought into the Doll's-house—a little boy and a little girl. They were not made of wood, like the common people; the one was china and the other wax. Their clothes were very beautiful, and made with great care. Indeed, they had every reason to be proud. The china doll's suit was of sky-blue silk, so the children called him "Little Boy Blue." As for the wax doll she was very fine indeed. She had a little hat, perched on the top of her head, which looked as if she was dressed to go out walking; but then she had a dress with a low-necked body and short sleeves, so that that clearly could not be. And her slippers were so delicate and thin, I know she could not have walked a step in them to save her life.

"Her name must be Miss Muffet," said the children, when they had thought about it for a long while.

Now these two dolls were of very high descent; they came, in fact, from the top of a Christmas tree. Their clothes were made in different pieces, and fitted their figures exactly; it was not surprising that they should look down on the wooden dolls, who were dressed in perfect *sacks*, all made in one piece, with just a string run through the middle to form a waist. They could not fraternise with them at all, and spoke to them as little as they could possibly help. Miss Muffet, indeed, seldom went inside the house, but passed most of her time sighing on the little green balcony in front of it.

"Why will you look so unhappy?" said Little Boy Blue to

her one day; "you know you could end it all in a minute, if
you liked. If you would only make up your mind to marry me,

58.—NEEDLEBOOK.　　　59.—NEEDLEBOOK.

60.—DETAIL OF 58.

you should be as happy as the day was long, and need never
speak to any of the wooden dolls again."

"They *are* common," Miss Muffet replied, with just the sus-
picion of a tear clouding her beautiful blue eyes; "they *are*

common, and I own I am very unhappy as I am; still the establishment is a large one, and not to be despised, and I could not
think of marrying unless I could have something similar."

Now, a house with six rooms and a staircase up the middle,
a green door with a brass knocker, and a fine balcony outside, is
not to be met with every day in the week.

61.—Easter Egg.

The little boy sighed, and was silent for a minute. Quite
suddenly, however, he cheered up.

" I know what I can do!" he cried. " I can't buy you a house
like that, it is true, but I'll *build* you a lovely one instead."

" Impossible!" answered Miss Muffet; " why will you talk of
absurdities like that? You could not build a house, to commence with, and if you could, it would take so long. We should
both be old by the time it was finished."

"That shows how little you know about it, my dear," said Boy Blue in a superior tone. "Take long to build a house! I'm a builder by trade, so I ought to know best. Now listen, and I'll tell you how it's done. Here, on our right, lies a lovely pack of cards—all the materials ready to hand. I shall run you up a house of them in no time, and it will be ready to live in to-night. Inside there will be the most beautiful pictures, and outside it will be all over a lovely blue, and you can't well be more artistic than that."

"I don't see how it's to be done," sighed Miss Muffet, but a slight smile stole over her face.

"I could almost build the house while I am talking about it," replied the china doll with some impatience; "but sit down here, and I will explain it to you. You first take two cards and stand them up so (like the gable of a cottage, or the letter V turned upside down). That, I grant you, is an anxious moment, but, once over, the next step is easy. You have to stand two cards, lengthways, each side of the gable, and then two crossing those again till you have a square all round the gable. Then comes another difficult part, when you lay two cards flat on the top of these, very carefully, so as not to knock the first part down. Then, feeling as if you dare scarcely breathe, for fear, you begin to build another story on the top of the two flat cards just in the same way. And as many stories as ever you like you can have—three, four, or five, and some people even had six!"

"How clever you are!" said Miss Muffet, "I understand it all perfectly. I think it will be a most elegant house, and one I could very well live in. Will you begin at once, Boy Blue? and I will sit and watch you while you work!"

And Miss Muffet retired from the balcony, came down the doll's house stairs, and out through the little green door with the brass knocker.

How pleased was Boy Blue when he saw her come out!

He kissed her little wax hand three times over, and then he tucked up his blue satin sleeves, and set to work to build the house.

Now there had been another wedding in the doll's house that same day, only as they were quite common people I forgot to mention it before. They were just two ordinary wooden dolls, of no consequence whatever, and they had set up with an establishment suited to their humble position in life—they had made their house out of a night-light box.

They heard the first sounds of building going on, and they both put their heads over the top of the night-light box and looked out.

Boy Blue had succeeded in fixing the gable, and was placing the four cards round its sides.

"Look what a beautiful house these people are going to have!" said the wooden doll, "all blue outside, and pictures within!"

"I don't think much of it yet," said the other wooden doll, who was the husband; perhaps he was jealous of the shiny blue house.

The first story was soon finished, and Little Boy Blue clapped his hands for joy.

"What a beautiful house!" cried his little wax bride, "so airy and light, so uncommon in style! Indeed, I am very much pleased with it, my dear."

"She'll be so proud there'll be no bearing with her," said the wooden doll-wife, with something not unlike a sob. "I wish my husband could have built me such a house!"

"It's no trouble at all to me," observed Little Boy Blue, "you know; I am a builder by trade," and he stood with his hands behind his back for a minute, resting, and admiring what he had done.

Then he began to work again, and with bated beath fixed up the second gable, and also the four cards by its sides.

91

"Two Dolls and a House of Cards."

62.
DOLL'S BONNET.

63.—DOLL'S COLLAR.

64.—DOLL'S HAT.

65.—DOLL'S HAT.

66.—DOLL'S BONNET.

67.—DOLL'S MANTILLA.

68.—DOLL'S COLLAR.

69.—DOLL'S PINAFORE.

70.—DOLL'S HAT.

71.—Doll's Shoe. 72.—Doll's Walking Boot. 73.—Doll's Shoe.

74.—Boy-Doll's Coat.

76.—Doll's Outdoor Jacket.

75.
Doll's Mantle.

77.—Doll's Sealskin Hat.

78.—Doll's Straw Hat.

93

" A house with two stories !" cried the night-light box dolls. " There is no end to some people's ambition."

" I am glad the wooden dolls see us," said Miss Muffet to herself, though she pretended not to notice their remarks ; " they will understand now what sort of establishment a person of my position expects."

At last the third story was safely completed, and the china doll stopped to take breath.

" Oh, how proud Miss Muffet will be !" said poor Mrs. Wooden Doll, bobbing her head up over the night-light box, " a house with three stories, and pictures inside ! When visitors come I

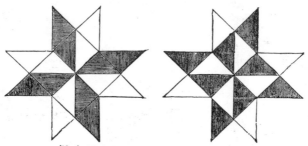

79 & 80.—DESIGNS IN PAPER FOLDING.

know what she will say. It will be, ' Which of my three rooms will you come into to-day ?' "

" All pride and vanity," said Mr. Wooden Doll. " I see nothing to admire in it at all."

A fourth story and a fifth rose, and the excitement became intense. All the dolls in the big red doll's house came out on to the balcony to stare. It was the happiest moment of Miss Muffet's life.

" How about a sixth story ?" said Little Boy Blue.

" I should like it," Miss Muffet replied.

" It has been done before now," said Boy Blue, rather doubtfully, " but I'm almost afraid of going farther."

"You know best," said she, with a little toss of her head "but if I were you I'd go on. A six-storied house would be charming—with all the dolls in the doll's house looking on."

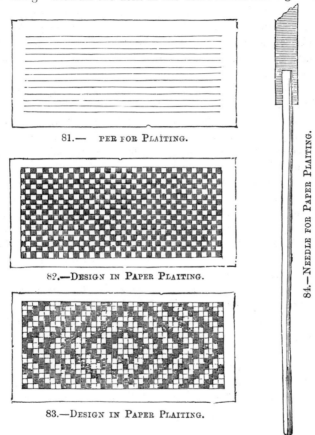

81.— PER FOR PLAITING.

82.—DESIGN IN PAPER PLAITING.

83.—DESIGN IN PAPER PLAITING.

84.—NEEDLE FOR PAPER PLAITING.

Alas for Boy Blue! He attempted the sixth gable; he placed the first two cards on their slippery foundation, another, and another by their sides, when his hand trembled a little, a sort of quiver went through the building, from roof to basement, and in one second, with a fearful crash, the whole house fell down, and lay in ruins at his feet.

Flat, flat, flat! Still and shapeless, so as not to be recognised. Pictures, and windows, and gables, all gone. Nothing could well be flatter. Talk of a pancake, why, a pancake is a promontory in comparison with the flatness of that house when it fell.

"I knew how it would be," said the night-light box doll. "No good ever came of trying to do too much."

The poor little builder! his eyes filled with tears; every one was laughing at him, and that is hard to bear; and some gave him good advice, and that is harder. He looked at his lady-love, but she would not meet his eye.

"You have humbled my pride," she said; "you have made me look ridiculous; I shall never love or trust you any more."

She heard all the wooden dolls laughing, she looked at the wreck upon the ground, then turned her back upon it all, and walked right into the garden with her head up in the air. There she sat down on a piece of stone, in a dreadful fit of the sulks. Now, sulks are bad for any sort of dolls, but they are fatal to a wax one, if she sits in the sun while she has them, that is; and that is precisely what happened to her. The sun shone, and shone, and she felt herself going, but she would not move; and first her colour, and then her nose, and then her arms, and the whole of her body, melted right away, till nothing was left of her but a little heap of wax upon the ground.

Alas, alas! for Miss Muffet. She had better have lived in the card-house, after all. It would not have lasted long, to be sure; but, after all, it was quite as durable as she was.

THE LADY'S LACE BOOK.

MODERN POINT LACE.

Introduction—Various kinds of Lace—Cravat-End in Modern Point—Imitation
of Old Point—Fan in Modern Lace—Cover for Pincushion—Cravat in
Brazilian Lace—Border in Renaissance-Work—Collar and Cuff in
Brazilian Lace.

To Barbara Uttman, the wife of a miner, in the Hartz
mountains of Saxony, has been attributed the invention of lace,
in 1561; but this is doubtful, as there are traces of its earlier
use as a pillow-made fabric. Many ancient specimens of lace
are worked entirely with the needle, and are marvellous examples
of skill, patience, and industry. The most ancient of all the
works falling under the general description of lace is nothing
otherwise than embroidery, such as is alluded to by secular
authors and in the sacred records of the Old Testament. The
many examples of this kind are, no doubt, familiar to our
readers.

Cut-work, drawn-work, darned netting and knotted lace were
extensively used in the Elizabethan age and later on. Family
portraits and monuments in churches furnish many interesting
illustrations of these.

Cut-work, as the term implies, was produced by cutting out
portions of a foundation of linen in patterns and working over
the edge with a buttonhole stitch, or else by overlaying reticu-
lated threads stretched on a frame, and so forming a pattern.

For drawn-work threads were drawn out of linen and worked
over with the needle, or the edges of the material unravelled,
and the threads woven together.

97

Knotting was another plan, and the darned netting was similar to modern work of the kind. Ancient examples of

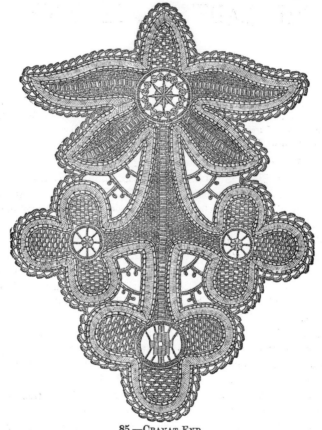

85.—CRAVAT-END.

darned netting exhibit figures of animals, birds, flowers, &c., frequently in squares with a border.

Most of the laces falling within the preceding enumeration are worked in designs of a geometrical form, deeply vandyked with

86.—INSERTION IN OLD POINT.

stars, crosses, wheels, triangles, flowers, and angular devices within them.

It must not be forgotten that there is a good deal of embroi-

dery used in the construction of these laces—that is, portions of the foundation not cut away are overlaid with thick needlework.

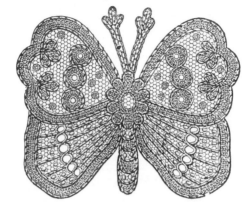

87.—LACE BUTTERFLY.

88.—LADY'S FAN.

Modern Maltese and Greek lace much resemble these old seventeenth-century fabrics.

Pincushion Cover.

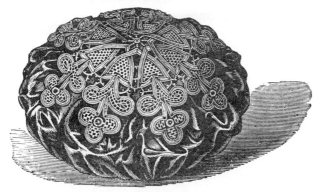

89.—Pincushion.

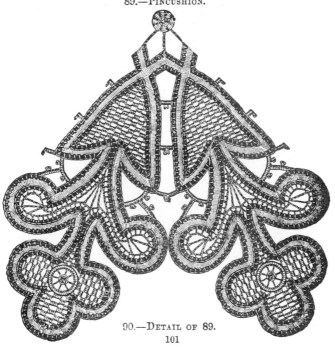

90.—Detail of 89.

101

Braid or "tape guipure" is that kind of lace whose design or pattern is formed of a continuous braid or tape of various widths, the interval being filled with a groundwork of fancy

91.—CRAVAT-END.

stitches, or else the lines of the patterns are merely connected by threads technically called bars, often decorated by little loops of thread. Much of the ancient lace of this description has been

102

reproduced with great success by ladies who have given attention to this branch of needlework.

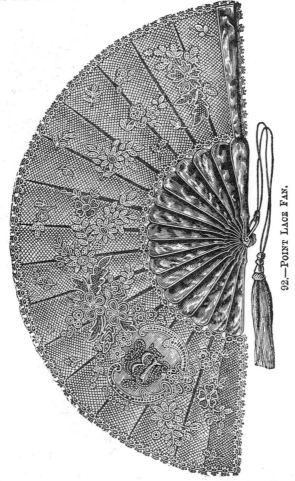

92.—POINT LACE FAN.

The best-known English laces are those of Honiton, Bucking-

hamshire, Northamptonshire, and Oxfordshire. Honiton lace
has obtained a deservedly high reputation, having been much

93.—DESIGN ENLARGED

patronised by Her Majesty the Queen and members of the Royal
Family; and through the influence exercised by the many inter-

national exhibitions of late years the fabric has been much improved in design and workmanship, and can now fairly com-

FROM No. 92.

pete with some of the best continental examples. For convenience' sake Honiton lace may be divided into two kinds—viz., point and appliqué—and this division will apply to most other descriptions of lace fabrics. It may not be strictly accurate, because most writers on lace have applied the term point to a

94—MONOGRAM FOR 92.

needle-made lace in contradistinction to that made on the pillow. For the present purpose, then, point may be described as a lace whose flowers or pattern are connected together by threads, already alluded to as bars, while appliqué is that whose flowers are applied or sewn on to a net ground. In both cases the·

95.—Rosette in Modern Lace.

96.—Lady's Cravat.

flowers or sprigs are made separately on the lace pillow; and previously to the invention of a machine-made net both net and sprigs were made on the pillow.

Of foreign laces the principal ones are Brussels, Valenciennes, Mechlin, Binche, Lille, Alençon, Chantilly, Venice.

One of the most beautiful kinds of these—viz., Venice point (known also as Rose point or raised point and Spanish point)—

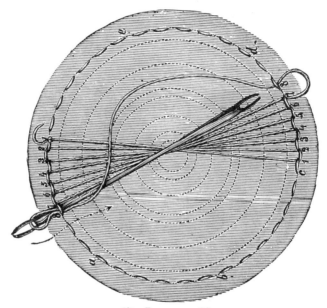

97.—Detail of 96.

has been rendered familiar to us by its reproduction, similar to that of the tape guipure mentioned previously. Venice point is formed of flowing lines, scrolls and flowers of very quaint forms in an infinite variety. The flowers are raised by an under padding of thread, and surrounded by delicate fringes; the connecting bars are pearled, and the fillings are of a most elaborate

kind : exquisite specimens of skilled and patient labour in needlework.

Brussels lace for beauty, fineness, and costliness takes a
leading place among the continental laces. The thread used is
of exquisite fineness, and the sprigs and scrolls forming the
pattern are bordered with a kind of cord. This lace not un-

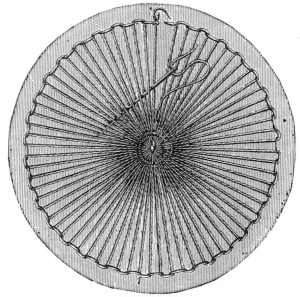

98.—DETAIL OF 96.

frequently tarnishes in consequence of a process of whitening in
its manufacture. The celebrity and beauty of Brussels lace is
the result of the combination of skilled workpeople in its production using both pillow and needle.

Valenciennes is a firm but beautiful lace, made entirely on
the pillow. The grounding net is often angular, but the flowers
are not usually corded.

109

Mechlin is a light and delicate lace, with its flowers and leaves surrounded with a flat thread; the net is frequently pow-·dered with small dots or flowers.

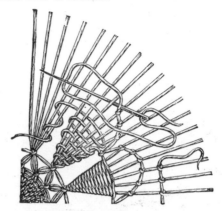

99.—Detail of 96.

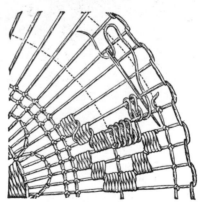

100.—Detail of 96.

The town of Binche produces a beautiful lace, whose **flowers** are both compact and fine.

Lille produces a light thread lace, with a ground of peculiar delicacy. The patterns are not very graceful, but rather stiff and angular, bordered with a thread. This lace has been sucsessfully imitated by some of our lace-producing English counties.

101.—DETAIL OF 96.

Alençon, point d'Alençon, is the most elegant of the lace fabrics, and owes its introduction into France to the celebrated Colbert, in 1660. This is a hand-made lace, worked entirely with the needle from a costly handspun thread. This, like that of Brussels, owes much of its beauty to the union of skilled

102.—Border in Renaissance-Work.

workers. Its designs are light and graceful and strongly bordered, which gives them an effective appearance.

103.—DETAIL OF 102.

104.—COVER FOR TOILET-CUSHION.

Chantilly is best known for its blonde laces, black and white, made with a silky thread. The flowers of the pattern

113

are usually worked with one of their sides thicker than the other.

No. 85. Cravat-End. Modern point lace. Materials: Nar-

105.—Lace Collar.

row white silk braid, white purse silk, and gold cord. Trace the design on tracing-paper, and work the wheels and lace stitches according to the illustration; then put in the Venetian bars in

114

buttonhole stitch, adding the purls. For the point de reprise the thread is taken across the work and filled up in the manner

106.—LACE CUFF, DETAIL OF 105.

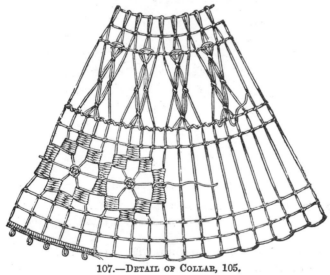

107.—DETAIL OF COLLAR, 105.

shown. The outer edge of the braid is finished with a pearl edging, and the gold thread sewn on with buttonhole stitches o white silk. Instead of the materials used in our model tho design may be worked with white point lace braid, embroidery cotton, and guipure cord.

No. 86. Imitation of Old Point. This design is worked on Brussels net with fine lace cotton and guipure cord. When the work is completed the net is cut away, leaving the pattern standing in relief. The design is suitable for cravat-ends.

No. 87. Butterfly in Modern Lace. Work the design on

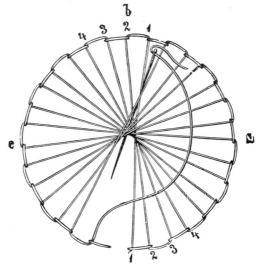

108.—DETAIL OF COLLAR, 105.

a ground of Brussels net, edging it with cord and close lace stitches forming a braid; then cut away the net from the outlines.

No. 88. Fan in Modern Lace. The sticks of this fan are ivory, with a point lace mounting worked on fine net. The stitches used are *point de toile, point de Bruxelles*, Sorrento wheels, and buttonhole stitch. A narrow purled braid edges the flowers.

Nos. 89 and 90. Pincushion. Circular cushion measuring about 6 inches in diameter and 3 in height. It is covered with blue satin arranged in puffings at the side, and has a cover of point lace. The puffing is cut out of a strip of satin 5 inches wide by 43 long. It is drawn up at each side over fine cord. Then trace from Illustration 90, which represents a fourth of the whole, the pattern on tracing-paper, and arrange on the latter a white silk point lace braid like that shown in the illustration. The separate parts of the pattern are joined together in the usual way with Venetian bars and purls. Then the

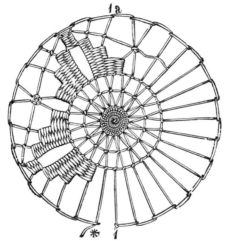

109.—Detail of Collar, 105.

various lace stitches and wheels are worked with white purse silk, and the braid is edged on each side with fine gold cord sewn on with fine white silk.

No. 91. Cravat-End in Modern Lace. Trace the design on paper, and then tack the braid in place. Two kinds of braid are required and fine lace cord. The design is filled up with Sorrento and English wheels, *point de filet, point Turque,* and twisted *brides.* The whole is edged with a cord joined to the design by means of long loops.

117

110.—Fan of Ivory and Lace.

112.—Detail of 111.

111.—Cravat of Indian Muslin.

118

Nos. 92 to 94. Fan in Modern Point Lace. White mother-

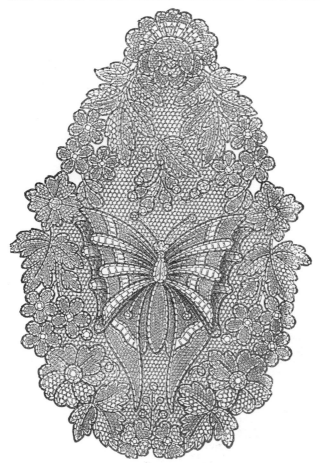

113.—DETAIL OF 111.

of-pearl fan covered with point lace, worked from the pattern given in No. 93. Trace the design on tracing-paper, over

114.—DETAIL OF 115.

115

Cruvat-End.

END.

116.—DETAIL OF 115.

121

which place fine net. For the monogram (No. 94) a ground of pale blue China silk is required; it is worked with gold thread and gold cord in satin and overcast stitch. Then arrange the braid according to the illustration, and work the veinings of the leaves. Between the leaves the net is darned, and the outer

117.—Detail of 115.

edge finished with a point lace braid. Blue silk cord and tassels complete the fan.

No. 95. Rosette in Modern Lace. This design is traced on paper, over which place fine net, and then proceed to fill in with lace cord and lace stitches. When the work is finished the net is cut away as shown in the illustration.

Nos. 96 to 101. Cravat-End. Brazilian sun pattern. This lacework was much admired at the recent Paris Exhibition, and

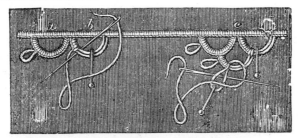

118.—Detail of 115.

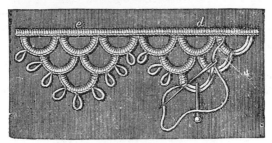

119.—Detail of 115.

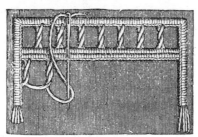

120.—Detail of 115.

is not difficult to learn. Trace on green oiled cloth the circular represented in No. 97, then divide the circle into six parts, as

shown on the illustration by the letters *a*, *b*, *c*, *d*, *e*, and 1.
These six parts are subdivided into six parts each, so that between
a and *d*, &c., there are 6 stitches. (See illustration.) These
36 stitches are only meant to support the lacework, and are
afterwards drawn out: they are fastened on the wrong side of
the cloth, then trace or press in the other lines necessary for the
lacework, and fill a very fine netting-needle with lace thread;
fasten the thread to the Fig. 1 as shown in the illustration,
stretch it across the circle to the Fig. 1 on the other side, and
bring it back to Fig. 2. When all the threads have been taken
across the circle except one, thread that into a sewing-needle,
and consulting No. 98, work the centre in point de reprise till
it is of the same size as the illustration, then turn to No 99, and
work across every 6 threads with one knotted stitch. In the next
row the 6 threads are divided, so that the knots occur in reversed
position. The same illustration also shows how each part of
the pattern is to be worked. Each row is separately fastened,
so that the one working thread which was left out at Fig. 1 is
filled up by degrees as each row is finished. No. 100 shows the
method of working the outer edge of the pattern. The traced
lines on the green cloth fix the position of the rows of work.
The smaller sun patterns shown on No. 101 can, by consulting
that illustration, be worked in a similar way. The outer edge
is then worked with a close row of buttonhole stitches and purls,
and the lace removed from the oiled cloth and sewn on to a
coloured scarf (No. 96).

Nos. 102 and 103. Border in Renaissance-Work. Trace the
design on tracing-paper, go over the outlines with fine lines of
thread, and fill up with the various lace stitches and wheels shown
in the illustration. The Venetian bars are worked with buttonhole stitch in the usual way, putting in the purls where required.
The outlines and the outer border are then worked over the five
lines of thread in close buttonhole stitch. The thickest outlines
are worked over two or more outlines together, as shown in

Illustration 103. When the work is completed it is carefully removed from the tracing-paper.

No. 104. Cover for Toilet-Cushion in Point Lace. Circular cushion scalloped round the edge and covered with pink satin, the sewing on of which is hidden by a pink cord. For the lace cover the design is traced on tracing-paper, and the outlines gone over with medallion-shaped and plain point lace braid. The lace stitches are then put on with fine thread, and the cushion is edged with narrow lace, the sewing on of which is hidden by a pearl edging.

Nos. 105 to 109. Collar and Cuff (Brazilian Lace). Draw with a compass upon the tracing-paper the outline of the rosettes given in No. 105. To make the work easier we give in other illustrations certain sections of it in a larger size—for instance, No. 108 shows how to put on the foundation threads for the rosette with the four vandykes, and No. 109 shows the lace stitches for the same rosette. The circle is first divided into four parts (see the letters), and the circumference is marked with 16 tacking-threads, as nearly as possible of equal length, as shown by No. 108. These stitches only serve as a help to the lace stitches, and are afterwards removed. Then the remaining outlines are traced with the compass, and the lacework is begun. For this part of the work thread an embroidery needle with thread about a yard long (see No. 108), and begin near the tacking-thread marked 1; go straight on, marking with the thread the diameter of the circle, so that your needle comes out at the opposite Fig. 1. Then pass the needle through the tacking-thread marked 2, and carry the thread across the circle to the opposite Fig. 2. The direction of each thread is marked on the circle with figures. When every thread except one has been traced in this way across the circle, then work round the centre of the circle, or *sol*, as the Brazilians call it, with a few stitches (see No. 108), and begin to fill up the vandykes in point de reprise, working over the foundation threads, as shown in

125

No. 109, till the close centre circle is large enough. Round this point de reprise every two threads are caught together by a knot, and this round is followed by a similar one, in which the

121.—SQUARE IN NETTING AND FLORENTINE EMBROIDERY.

knots occur in reversed position. In the third knotted round a knot is worked over every thread; and now it must be observed that every round of the pattern is complete in itself, and that the threads which are still wanting between the centre and the outside tacking-threads near Fig. 1 are put in as the work proceeds, by carrying the foundation thread (see No. 109) through the tacking-thread marked with *, by Fig. 1. The same illustration shows (still in enlarged size) the working of the point de reprise and punto tirato knots. When the centre circle of a

122.—Square in Netted Guipure.

rosette is finished prepare the outer part in the same way, according to No. 107. The other rosettes and the connecting pattern are done in a similar way, and the outer edge of all the rosettes is worked in close buttonhole stitch, purls being introduced, as shown in the illustration. The collar and cuffs, which are embroidered in the same manner, are then sewn on to a ground of fine lawn like an appliqué design, the ground being cut away from under the work close to the buttonhole stitches. (See Nos. 105 and 106.)

123.—SQUARE IN GUIPURE FOR COVERS.

No. 110. Fan of Ivory and Imitation of Real Lace. Our illustration represents an ivory fan with folding part of pale blue satin. The satin is covered with lace. Take, as the foundation for the lacework, a piece of stiff paper, over which

128

place mull muslin. Then trace the design on blue card, cut out the separate patterns, and fasten them on to the muslin and paper. The connecting bars are next worked, and the close part of the patterns is filled up in point de toile, the parts which

124.—SQUARE FOR ANTIMACASSAR (Netted Guipure).

imitate coarse net with double thread. The muslin is then cut away and the lace stitches and purls put in. When the embroidery is finished cut away all the ground which can be removed, and draw out any threads of muslin which remain.

Nos. 111 to 113. Imitation Point Lace. On the ends of this

129

cravat of India muslin is an appliqué of Brussels net, embroidered in imitation of old point lace. Trace the design given in the original size in Nos. 112 and 113 on to tracing-paper, over which place Brussels net, and go over the outlines with fine

125.—Antimacassar (Satin-Stitch and Guipure).

guipure cord and buttonhole stitches of fine thread. The raised spots are then put in and the lace stitches worked. For the open-worked parts in the butterflies' wings and rosettes the thread is worked in overcast stitch, and the net is cut away from beneath the work.

126.—DETAIL OF 125

127.—DETAIL OF 125.

Nos. 114 to 120. Designs for Cravat-Ends, &c. These designs are embroidered in guipure and point lace, with very fine guipure cord and overcast stitch of lace thread. Illustration 114 shows the close buttonhole stitch which forms the ground of the designs. Illustration 116 shows the stitch point de poste. Nos. 118 & 119 give the purls. The embroidery when completed is taken off the ground of tracing-paper, and sewn on to coloured silk.

128.—DETAIL OF 125.

133

GUIPURE D'ART.

No. 121. Square (Netting and Florentine Embroidery). The ground is of plain netting, filled up with point de toile, point de reprise, and point d'esprit. The separate vandykes of the centre star are worked in guipure needlework. The bars are filled up in point de reprise.

No. 122. Squares in Netted Guipure. The ground of straight netting is filled up with point de toile and point d'esprit. For the vandykes between the point d'esprit pass the thread over the two vertical threads and the horizontal ones between them until a triangle is formed; the triangles meeting, form a square at the corners and in the centre of the work. The leaf pattern is worked with black silk in buttonhole stitch, and the tendrils filled up in point de reprise.

No. 123 is worked on a ground of straight netting in point de toile, wheels and buttonhole stitch, and point de reprise. The netted ground is cut away in the buttonhole squares.

No. 124 is worked on a ground of straight netting in point de soie and in point de reprise. The wheels are worked with crosswise bars and overcast, and filled up with thread in various lace stitches. The squares are put together with buttonhole stitch.

Nos. 125 to 128. Chair Back (Satin Stitch and Netted Guipure). Ground of white linen gauze 19 inches square, with centre square of cream-coloured netting worked with split filoselle. The design for the latter is given in Illustration 126, which represents half the square; it is worked in straight netting with a double thread of split filoselle over a mesh less than half an inch wide, and filled up in point de toile and point d'esprit, while the 2nd and 3rd rows of holes from the outer edge are worked with the filoselle as shown in Illustration 126. The centre pattern with the wheel is filled up in point de toile, worked over with satin stitch, and bars in point de reprise. The close patterns are outlined with several loose threads of silk sewn on with overcast stitches. The stems of the leaves, worked in point de reprise, are wound round with purse stitch of the same silk. When the completed square has been sewn on to the linen gauze with close buttonhole stitch, a second row of the same stitch is worked close to the other, each stitch taking in 3 threads of the gauze in height, and the ground is then cut away from the netted guipure. For the open-work pattern, round this centre square leave 7 threads, draw out 3 times alternately 10 threads and leave 4, then draw out 10. Then leave 96 threads, and 3 times alternately draw out 10, leave 4, and draw out 10. For the corner squares, see Illustration 128, and for the side oblong patterns, Illustration 127. These designs are worked in satin or buttonhole stitch with cream-coloured silk, filled up with plain or chain stitch. Every row of the open-work pattern is worked by crossing every 6 of the 4 threads left standing, the needle being threaded with cream-coloured silk, the corners where the threads cross being worked according to the illustration. Round the outer row of open-work the linen gauze is hemmed, and a frill of lace is added, as shown in Illustration 125.

Nos. 129 & 134 to 137. Watch-Stand. Frame of black polished cane, with oval medallion, edged with gold beading. The watch rests against a wadded surface, covered with blue satin, and small square of lace. Below a cradle-shaped tray, covered *en suite*, to receive jewellery. The lace cover and lambrequin

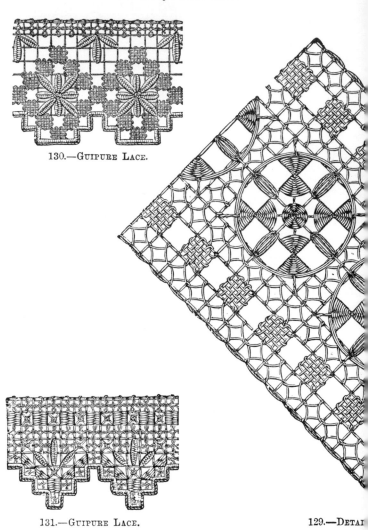

130.—GUIPURE LACE.

131.—GUIPURE LACE.

129.—DETAI

132.—GUIPURE EDGING.

133.—GUIPURE EDGING.

OF 134.

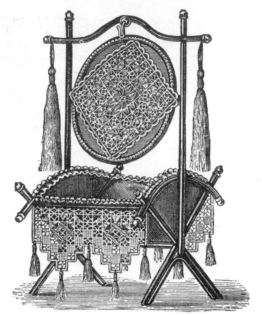

134.—WATCH-STAND.

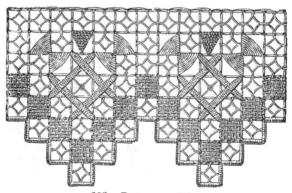

135.—DETAIL OF 134.

136.—DETAIL OF 134.

137.—DETAIL OF 134.

are worked in netted guipure. (See Illustrations 129 and

138.—Design for a Rochet.

130.—Lace Border for a Rochet.

136.) A ground of straight netting is filled up with point

de toile, point de reprise, and point d'esprit, and is edged

140.--DESIGN FOR A ROCHET.

141.--DESIGN FOR A ROCHET.

round with two rows of tatting.   Four tatted stitches (double)
are worked in each netted stitch.   For the 2nd row the thread

is arranged in loops round the scallops, and then 5 tatted stitches are worked in each loop. Nos. 135 and 136 illustrate the edgings used. Tassels of blue silk.

Nos. 130 to 133. Guipure Lace Edgings. No. 130 is worked on a ground of straight netting in point de toile, point d'esprit, and point de reprise. The edge is buttonholed and the netting then cut away. No. 131 is worked in point d'esprit, point de reprise, and point de feston, with an edge like No. 132. No. 132

142.—Design for a Rochet.

is in point de reprise, point d'esprit, and point de toile with wheels in addition. No. 133 is in point d'esprit, point de toile, and point de reprise, with dots in the open squares.

Nos. 138 to 143. The Rochet should be of fine lawn or batiste, with guipure embroidery, for which we give several designs. The Venetian bars are worked in the usual way, the outlines are edged with buttonhole stitch, and the vandykes filled up in point de reprise. The ground is then cut away from the embroidery, as the illustration directs.

No. 144. Squares for Chair-Backs, &c. Ground of straight netting worked with point de toile and wheels.

No. 145. Square in Guipure d'Art. Ground of straight netting worked in point de toile and point de feston.

Nos. 146 to 148. Child's Collar (Guipure Embroidery). Collar of fine lawn turned down and worked with an open hem; an edging of guipure lace is sewn round the outer edge of the collar. The pattern of the lace must be taken from the repre-

143.—DESIGN FOR A ROCHET.

sentation given on a small scale in No. 146, and from the Illustrations 147 and 148. The tracing-paper is then sewn on to the waxed cloth, and double lines of thread are carried along the two lines which mark the upper and lower edge of the square, and are fastened down with overcast stitches of fine thread. The double threads are then worked in point de reprise, and then the straight lines on the side of each separate square. The inner squares are next worked in the same way. The working thread is then carried across for the bars which cross

143

144.—SQUARE FOR CHAIR-BACKS, &c.

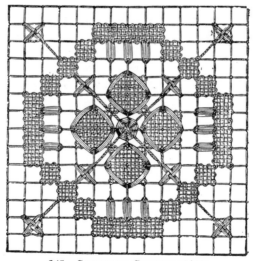

145.—SQUARE IN GUIPURE D'ART.

each other, and forms the vertical and horizontal lines of the pattern of four leaves. For each leaf, see No. 147 ; begin from the centre, and work a row of open buttonhole stitches, and then another row on the other side of the foundation thread, putting in the needle between two stitches of the former row. In the 3rd row of the leaf a buttonhole stitch is worked in every 3rd stitch of the 2nd row, and each stitch is once more wound

146.—CHILD'S COLLAR.

round with the working thread. In the last row 3 buttonhole stitches are worked in every stitch of the preceding row, with purls, which should be worked over a pin, as shown in No. 147. When the leaf pattern is finished, the working thread should be carried on to the corners of the square, and overcast. The scallops are then carried across the bars and worked over in buttonhole stitch, as shown in No. 147, the purls being added according to the same illustration. The squares shown in No. 148 and the scallops round the outer edge are worked in the same manner. The close leaves are worked in interlacing buttonhole stitch, and joined together by scallops, also worked

147.—DETAIL OF 146.

in buttonhole stitch. The completed lace is then added to the collar, as shown in the illustration.

No. 149. Border in Netted Guipure. The ground is of plain netting, filled up in point de toile and point d'esprit. The

squares of point de toile are embroidered with little blossoms of
black floss silk, and with crescent-shaped bars of white thread
in overcast stitch. The loose bars are filled up in point de
reprise. Round the outer edge are buttonhole stitches and
scallops of black silk with purls at intervals.

No. 150. Pincushion. Square pincushion of blue satin, with
cover in netted guipure and ruching of blue satin ribbon,

148.—DETAIL OF 146.

arranged in box pleats. For the square a netted ground of
écru-coloured thread, filled up with point de toile, point de
reprise, and point d'esprit, according to Illustration 150.

Nos. 151 to 154. Antimacassar (Netted Guipure & Embroidery).
This consists of squares of netted guipure and of linen gauze; the
latter squares measure about 11 inches wide, and they are turned
down 1 inch and worked with an open hem. Transfer the
pattern on to the centre square and on to the corner squares,

and work the embroidery in overcast, knotted, and satin stitch with red filoselle. The guipure squares are worked on a ground of straight netting from the designs given in Illustrations 152 and 153 in point de toile and point d'esprit. The raised leaves

149.—BORDER IN NETTED GUIPURE.

are worked in point de reprise, and the connecting bars in cordonnet stitch. The wheels are then worked and the separate patterns outlined with fourfold thread. The squares are then sewn together on the wrong side in the position shown in Illustration 151, and the antimacassar is edged with guipure lace

148

netted in the same pattern as that shown in Illustration 154. The lace is then edged with buttonhole stitches, and the netting is cut away from the work.

No. 155. Cravat-End. This design is worked upon a ground of straight netting, and is filled up with the same material (lace thread) in point de toile, point d'esprit, and point de reprise. Round the close stripe worked in point de toile are rows of chain stitch of blue and red silk. The vandykes round the outer edge are worked in buttonhole stitch, the ground being cut away between each vandyke.

No. 156. Sofa-Cushion (Netted Guipure). Square cushion covered with claret-coloured velvet, and edged round with a double box-pleated frill of claret-coloured satin ribbon, two inches wide. Along the upper frill a thick gold cord is sewn on with overcast stitches of gold-coloured silk. The centre square on the upper side of the cushion is worked on a ground of straight netting worked with gold-coloured purse silk, and filled up in point de toile, point de reprise, and point d'esprit, with similar silk and with gold thread. The border is worked with raised spots of loops, and patterns filled up in point de toile, and is finished round the outer edge with close buttonhole stitch.

Nos. 157 and 158. Squares in Guipure d'Art. These pretty designs are worked on straight netting in point d'esprit, point de toile, buttonhole stitches, and point de reprise, with fillings of wheels in both. The ground is cut away in both patterns, but especially in No. 158.

Nos. 159 to 161. Design for Quilts. This is of quilted blue silk, with an écru tussore border trimmed with guipure lace and insertion. The insertion No. 160 is worked in point de toile, point de reprise, point d'esprit, point de feston, and wheels. The same stitches are used in the lace edging (No. 161), with the exception of the point de feston.

PUNTO TIRATO.

Designs in Punto Tirato—Towels in Punto Tirato—Bows for the Neck—
Quilt — Sofa-Cushion — Chair-Back — Négligé-Case — Square in Punto
Tirato—Designs for Afternoon Tea-Cloths—Antimacassars.

Nos. 162 and 163. Table-Cover. This cover has a centre of
plain linen, and round the outer edge an open-worked border as
follows :—Leave about 6 inches for the fringe, and then alter-

150.—Pincushion.

nately draw out both ways of the stuff 20 threads, and leave 40.
Cut the ends partly away from the centre as shown in illustration, then for a bar work 1 buttonhole stitch over 10 threads
(see Illustration No. 163), and carry the working thread on to
next bar, crossing the threads where they meet in the open
square. In the centre of the close squares work an eyelet-hole
in buttonhole stitch. Round the linen centre leave 10 threads,
draw out one, and work a close row of buttonhole stitch over

the 10 threads, then draw together the centre of each 5 button-hole stitches with 1 plain stitch, carrying the working thread along the wrong side. The fringe is then unravelled and knotted.

151.—ANTIMACASSAR (Netted Guipure and Embroidery).

No. 164. Open-work Pattern Square for Antimacassars. On a square of guipure gauze work the design as follows :—At a little distance from the edge draw out 10 threads and leave 3, draw out 7, leave 3, draw out 10. Thread a needle with brown thread, and in the broader stripes join every 4 threads by passing the third and fourth thread under the first and second.

152.—Detail of 151.

In the narrower stripe work every 2 threads in the same way. Between the stripes work a row of tent stitch with brown thread. This should be done before drawing out any threads, or it will be found difficult to keep the work in place. Each stitch takes in 2 threads wide and 1 high of the ground.

153.—DETAIL OF 151.

Nos. 165 and 166. Towel (Embroidery and Punto Tirato). Narrow towel of coarse white holland, with monogram at one end and a pattern in punto tirato at each end. Below the border the ground is fringed out and knotted as shown in the illustration. Before beginning this border the ground has to be unravelled in squares by drawing out 4 threads long and 4 wide. Then for the centre part of the border draw out 12 sets of threads and work the 2 nearest sets right and left from the open part with cross stitches of white thread as shown in Illustration 166. Then for the centre of the border, take 9 sets of thread together and fill them up, beginning the centre in

154.—DETAIL OF 151.

point de reprise, by taking thread No. 2 and working over 3 sets of threads in succession. Then cross threads No. 1 and No. 2; work a knot round the next 3 sets of threads above for another pattern, wind it round, as shown by No. 3, beginning from the centre and work a similar pattern. Continue in this way with threads Nos. 4 and 5, but in the centre vandyke instead of filling up 9, only fill up 3 sets of threads in 3 repetitions. Then take thread No. 6 and wind round thread No. 1, working the wheels at the crossing points, as shown in Illustration 166. For the rest of the border, close to the 2 rows of cross stitches, draw out 2 sets of threads, and then work 2 more rows of cross stitch, and over every 2 sets of threads left standing work a punto-tirato knot. Then draw out 1 set of threads and work round the next 2 sets reverse stitches of white thread. For the latter,

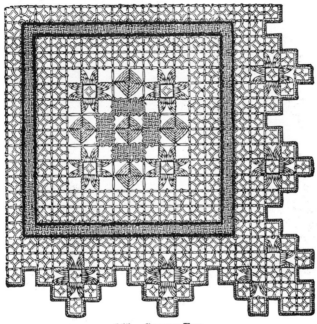

155.—CRAVAT-END.

pass the needle alternately from left to right, horizontally across the 2 sets of threads to the left, then below the one on the right towards the outside, work a stitch in a slanting direction and so on. On the other side of the border the horizontal and diagonal stitches meet reversed, each over 3 sets of threads. The hem along the long way of the towel is edged by a narrow border punto tirato. The monogram is worked with white embroidery cotton in satin, overcast, and plain stitch. When the embroidery is completed, unravel the ground and knot the fringe according to Illustration 165.

No. 167. Border for Antimacassar, &c. (Punto Tirato.) The design is worked on a ground of coarse, loosely-woven lawn in

156.—SOFA-CUSHION.

punto tirato with white purse silk. Every 4th thread is drawn out horizontally and vertically. Then for the centre draw out 10 sets of threads, and sew round every 2 sets of thread on the margin as follows:—Overcast the *left* of 2 sets of threads horizontally, pass the thread through the hole formed by drawing out the 4th thread, overcast horizontally the *right* of the 2 sets of threads, and carry the thread aslant (see illustration) from below upwards, towards the outside of the work. Between

156

every 2 of these patterns one set of threads is drawn out. For the close patterns, fill up every 8 of the horizontal sets of threads, overcasting first 2, then 4, and then 6 sets of threads. A separate working thread is required for each close pattern. When this point de reprise work is complete, work the scalloped lines in punto tirato, as shown in the illustration, taking in every 2 sets of threads together.

157.—SQUARE FOR ANTIMACASSAR.

Nos. 168 and 169. Bow for the Neck. This bow is worked with coloured filoselle on crossway pieces of linen gauze. Consult the pattern given in No. 168, which is worked as follows in cross stitch and open-work. For the latter, draw out 8 threads, and cross every 4 with white thread as shown in the illustration. Leaving 4 threads, work round the edge a row of buttonhole stitches with olive-green silk, and cut away the projecting ground. Then arrange the gauze as shown in No. 169, and trim with Russian lace.

Nos. 170 and 171. Bow for the Neck. See the pattern given in No. 170. For the open-work pattern draw out 6 threads; of the threads left standing, cross every 4 with the working thread of fine cotton, and work round 2 of these threads with purse stitches; then on the other side take 2 more threads, catch them together with the preceding 2, and continue in the same manner. The cross-stitch pattern is worked with blue

158.—SQUARE FOR ANTIMACASSAR.

and fawn-coloured silks. Lastly, the outer edge is hemmed and trimmed with Russian lace.

Nos. 172 to 175. Quilt and Cover (Punto Tirato). The quilt is made of blue cashmere, wadded and quilted with silk of the same colour. Cover of linen, with open-worked patterns above the hem. The hem is nearly four inches wide, and is worked in a simple open-hem pattern, like that shown in Nos. 174 and 175, the former showing the work from left to right, and the latter from right to left. The linen is drawn

ready for the punto tirato, and each edge of the pattern is
strengthened by a row of open-hem stitching. For the wider
punto tirato pattern consult No. 173, and join every 2 sets of
threads in a punto tirato knot. The close pattern is worked
over 4 sets of threads in point de reprise as far as the centre of

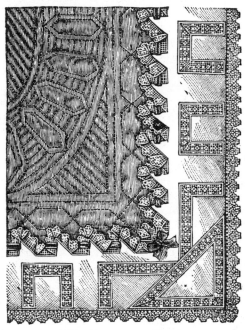

159.—Design for Quilts.

the pattern, where a slender connecting line is worked, taking
in each set of threads separately, and then the pattern is
finished as it was begun, in point de reprise. In the first row
of the narrower pattern join every 2 sets of threads with a
punto tirato knot, and work the second row in the same way,
but in reversed position.

Nos. 176 to 180. Sofa Cushion (Netting and Punto Tirato). Square cushion, covered with old-gold silk brocade first, and then with coarse white holland, embroidered in netted guipure and punto tirato with old-gold and maize purse silk.

160.—DETAIL OF 159.

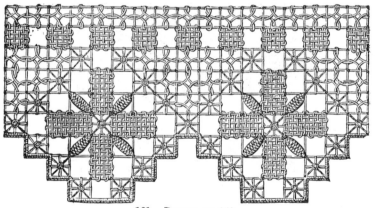

161.—DETAIL OF 159.

Round the cushion is an edging of guipure lace. The punto tirato pattern is begun with the centre square (see No. 178), which represents it in the original size. Draw out 4 threads both ways of the holland, then 6 times alternately leave 4 threads, draw out 4 threads until there are **7 rows of holes** formed, the threads being only partially drawn out and cut close with sharp scissors, the marginal edges being then worked with wide purse stitches of maize silk. (See No. 178.) Then fill up the 4 threads left between the holes in point de reprise with the same silk, taking in 2 threads to each stitch. The open squares

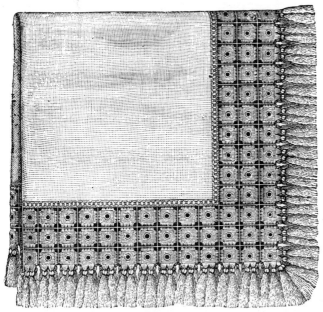

162.—TABLE-COVER.

are next crossed by overcast bars crossed in the centre. Then to make a firm edge to this square, work over 4 threads of the holland with 4 double threads of silk so that there are 4 stitches to each square both ways of the holland, and then, with old-gold silk, work a row of close buttonhole stitches, each stitch taking in 4 threads high. For the corner squares in guipure embroidery go over the outline several times to and fro, the width of the border of close buttonhole stitch, and cut away the ground between each square. Then place the squares over the tracing-paper on which the pattern shown in No. 177 has been already drawn. Now with old-gold silk (double thread) work across the square, fastening the stitches in the overcast margin, and filling up in point de reprise. The bars, which start from the corners, are worked in the same way and joined where they

163.—DETAIL OF 162.

cross in the centre with the same silk. Then work over the outlines of the circles and curved bars (see No. 177), and cover them with close buttonhole stitches. The outer circle is worked with 3 rows of buttonhole stitches, and then the vandyked and overcast bars are worked in the corners. Last of all the square is outlined in buttonhole stitch, like the preceding in No. 178. For the close square see No. 179, and having drawn out 4 threads and left 4 alternately, work according to illustration in point de reprise and buttonhole stitch, but in turning the thread join it on to the buttonhole stitches of the guipure squares.

A new thread is required for the centre pattern of these squares. The work, when so far completed, is worked round in the same manner as the centre square, and then, for the narrow edge of the border, of which No. 180 represents a corner, worked over 12 threads of holland as follows:—Take 4 threads upon the

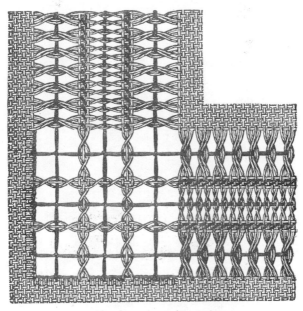

164.—SQUARE FOR ANTIMACASSARS.

needle, threaded with brown gold filoselle, and carry the filoselle straight down across 12 threads, take up 4 more threads and carry the filoselle upwards over 12 threads, and so on. Then lay two horizontal threads of the filoselle across the vertical ones and cross them with gold thread as follows:—Take 4 threads on the needle and carry the gold thread across the silk, plaiting it in and out as it were, as the illustration shows; take

up 4 more threads and continue in the same way. Then work
two rows like that worked round the centre square, and prepare
the holland for the broader part of the border as follows:—
Draw out 4 threads, leave 5 times alternately 4 threads, draw

165.—TOWEL.

out 4, so as to leave 6 rows of holes. The spaces are then filled
up with maize silk, according to No. 180, in point de toile and
point de reprise, and the outer edge is worked with the same
silk like the outer edge of the centre square. The cover is
then finished with a border of guipure lace, the patterns of
which have been worked with yellow silk.

Nos. 181 and 182. Designs for Towels, &c. The patterns are marked on linen gauze with glacé thread of different thicknesses. In No. 182 the squares are worked in satin stitch with double thread over 6 threads high and 4 broad, and the 3 raised lines

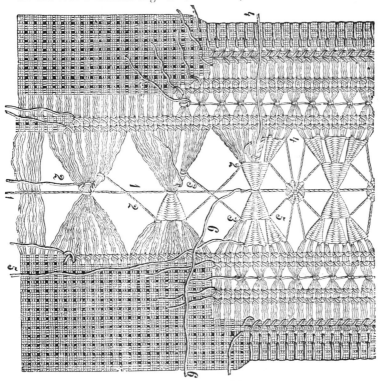

166.—Detail of 165.

in purse stitch over 2 threads. In the open-worked rows (see No. 182) * have the needle filled with fine thread, take up 6 threads vertically, pass the needle horizontally across 4 threads to the right, make a cross stitch over 4 threads, and carry on

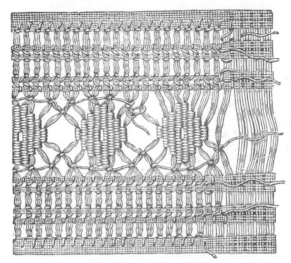

167.—BORDER FOR ANTIMACASSARS.

168.—DETAIL OF 169.

169.—BOW FOR THE NECK.

170.—DETAIL OF 171.

171.—BOW FOR THE NECK.

172.—QUILT.

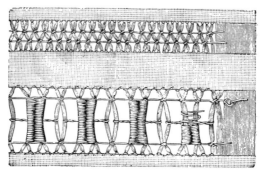

173.—DETAIL OF 172.

the working thread along the wrong side of the work. Repeat

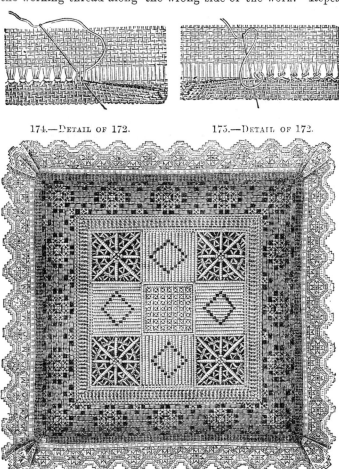

174.—DETAIL OF 172.   175.—DETAIL OF 172.

176.—SOFA-CUSHION IN PUNTO TIRATO.

from *. In No. 181 the open-worked rows are made in the

same way as those just described, and the rest of the work is
done in satin stitch.

Nos. 183 and 184. Antimacassar (Cross Stitch and **Punto**
Tirato). Ground of écru-coloured linen gauze, 24 inches long
by 11 wide, and woven with 7 close and 8 open stripes. The
latter have four woven lines of reseda thread, and are embroidered down the centre with reseda silk in feather-stitch. The

177.—Detail of 176.

2nd, 3rd, 5th, and 6th of the close stripes are worked in cross
stitch (see No. 184), with 2 shades of pink, reseda, and brown
silk. The 1st, 4th, and 7th stripes have 14 threads drawn
out in the centre, and 3 left standing on each side. These
centre threads are then worked in punto tirato, as shown in
Illustration 184, each 4 being joined together at a little distance
from the 3 threads left standing. The needle is threaded with

one of the threads drawn out, and two rows of knots are worked on each side of the stripe. The linen gauze is turned down in a hem, and feather-stitched round with reseda silk. A frill of écru-coloured torchon lace is sewn round the edge.

Nos. 185 and 186. Négligé-Case. Case of fine lawn embroidered in front with chain stitching of blue thread and trimmed with Russian lace and insertion. For the case and

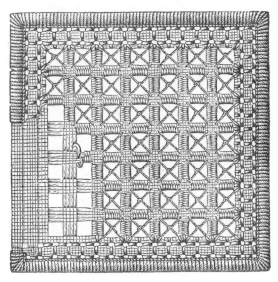

178.—DETAIL OF 176.

flap, cut out of fine lawn a straight piece 32 inches long by 18 wide, and round it at one of the narrow ends, sloping downward from the centre. For the open-work pattern consult No. 186, and draw out 52 threads the long and broad way, leaving 52 untouched; repeat as often as necessary, and then draw out (both ways) every 13th thread of the 52 left in. The edge of the open-work is worked in buttonhole stitch, each stitch taking in 13 threads of the ground. Then work the open-work pattern as shown in No. 186, in overcast stitch, one stitch taking in two of the stripes formed of six loose threads; the pattern must occur in reversed position. The last row of these squares is worked with close buttonhole stitch. Then fill up the open space by taking the thread across them diagonally and working the centres in overcast stitch and point de reprise.

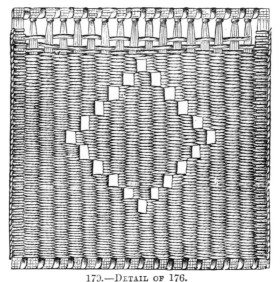

179.—DETAIL OF 176.

The squares from which the threads have not been drawn are worked with blue thread in buttonhole stitch, cross stitch, and point russe. When the open-work is completed sew on a band of Russian insertion, cutting away the ground from underneath. Both the lace and insertion are sewn on to the ground with buttonhole stitches of pale blue, and the same colour is used to embroider the patterns in point russe. The back of the case is then sewn to the front along each side underneath the lace, and the flap is bound with a narrow band of cambric and fastened to the bag with button and buttonhole.

Nos. 187 to 190. Designs for Afternoon Tea-Cloths, &c.

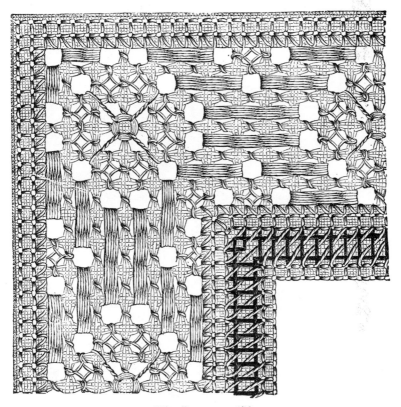

180.—Detail of 176.

If these designs are intended for borders the edges must be strengthened with close buttonhole stitch. The ground should be of medium coarseness in holland or crash. For No. 187

draw out 9 threads lengthways and across, and stitch round the squares, taking in 3 threads with every stitch. For No. 188, after working the squares in point d'esprit, fill in the wheels. No. 189. Draw out vertically and horizontally 10 threads and leave 10 threads. The margin must be worked with white thread in close buttonhole stitch. The 5 threads left undrawn are then worked in point d'esprit and overcast stitch with white thread. (See illustration.) No. 190. Alternately draw out 10

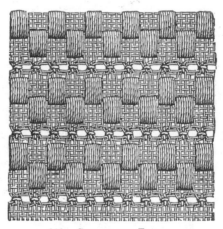

181.—Square for Towel.

threads and leave 4. Work round the margin with buttonhole stitches of white thread. The open-worked pattern is worked with blue thread as follows :—In the centre of the 4 threads work 4 buttonhole stitches and carry on the thread in a slanting direction to the next 4. In the return row bring the thread back in the same direction and wind it round the connecting thread. (See illustration.) The stitches at the crossing points are put in with blue thread in point de reprise.

Nos. 191 and 192. Sections of Antimacassars (Punto Tirato

and Satin Stitch). Ground of écru-coloured Russian canvas, embroidered with squares of red, blue, and white purse silk, in satin stitch. For the open-work pattern proceed as follows. Draw out the requisite number of threads and fasten on a needleful of écru-coloured purse silk, wind round the cut threads of the narrow edge of the opening with close overcast stitches of écru-coloured silk. Then darn the next 5 threads, and work the bar in overcast stitch and point de reprise.

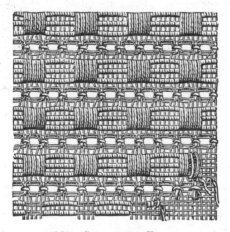

182.—Square for Towel.

Round the outer edge the work is embroidered with blue silk in buttonhole stitch, and the fringe is knotted as follows :—Every 12 threads of canvas is wound round 6 times with écru-coloured silk, then divide the threads and wind them round as before, but in reversed position. The ends of thread are then cut level. No. 192. For the deep border of this pattern the canvas is fringed out to the required length and breadth, and the bars of écru-coloured silk are worked according to illustration in overcast stitch and point de reprise. The open-worked pattern is

175

then edged round with buttonhole silk over four threads, and

183.—ANTIMACASSAR (Cross-Stitch and Punto Tirato.)

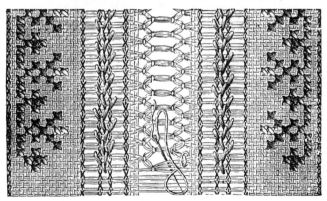

184.—DETAIL OF 183.

8 threads in height. The narrow open-worked pattern is effected

185.—NÉGLIGÉ-CASE.

186.—DETAIL OF 185.

in a similar way. The open-work squares are filled up in a kind of netted stitch, with the leaf pattern in point de reprise and wheels in lace stitch. The rest of the embroidery is worked in

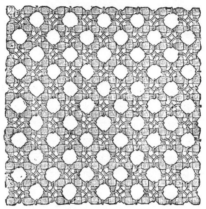

187.—Pattern for Tea-Cloth.

188.—Pattern for Tea-Cloth.

satin and overcast stitch with écru-coloured silk. For the fringe, cross every six threads and knot them together, adding new threads as usual at the corners.

Nos. 193 to 197. Sofa-Cushion (Punto Tirato). Square cushion covered with écru or pale yellow linen, not too fine, and

189.—DESIGN FOR TEA-CLOTH.

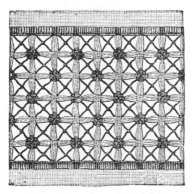

190.—DESIGN FOR TEA-CLOTH.

easily counted as to the strands. Begin in the corner with medium purse silk as follows :—At the point marked *a*, No. 196, draw out 3 vertical and 3 horizontal threads, not quite to the end of the ground, and about 4 inches long.   Leave 3 threads,

191.—SECTION OF ANTIMACASSAR (Satin-Stitch).

draw out 3 more threads as before, and repeat, until, as Illustration 196 shows, there are 5 rows of holes; then at the point marked *b* cut 27 threads of the ground straight through, and

192.—Section of Antimacassar (Satin-Stitch).

unravel them for $2\frac{1}{2}$ inches below the incision, leaving the outer edge untouched, then leave 3 threads remaining (see letter *c*),

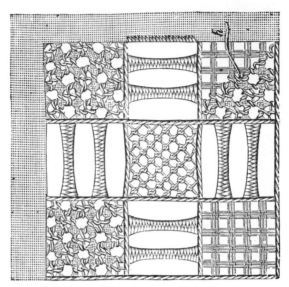

193.—DETAIL OF 197.

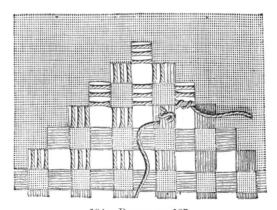

194.—DETAIL OF 197.

Detail of Sofa-Cushion.

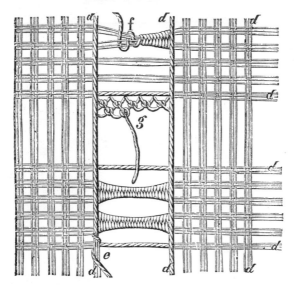

195.—DETAIL OF 197.

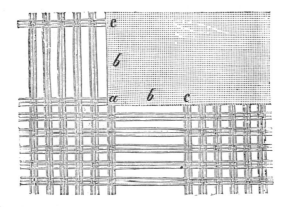

196.—DETAIL OF 197.

draw out 3 more threads, and proceed in the way above described till a square is prepared. The punto tirato is then begun from

the point marked *d* in Illustration 195, over-casting the threads and making them firm as shown at *e;* then fill up the 3 threads, taking 2 at a time and working according to *f* in point de reprise so as to form 2 graduated bars like those between *e* and *g.* The free square is then filled up in lace stitch. The punto tirato in the trellis-patterned squares is worked according to Illustration 193, letter *h.* The working thread should not be very tightly drawn. When the border has been sewn on in purse silk work round a row of satin and Holbein stitch as shown in Illustration 197. For the centre square consult Illustration 194. Begin from the centre by drawing out 9 threads and leaving 9 to the right and 9 to the left, continue as shown in the illustration, and work the punto tirato by overcasting every 3 threads; then

197.—SOFA

work round the completed diamond
and Holbein work. The cover should

a border of satin stitch
be placed over a cushion
of bright-coloured satin
and edged with cord and
tassels to match the satin
ground.

Nos. 198 to 201.
Afternoon Tea - Cloth.
Square ground of grey
Java canvas, embroidered
with coloured filoselle in
double satin stitch and
Holbein work. The
flowers are embroidered
with two shades of red,
and the tendrils and
borders with olive green
and black. In the centre
are gold spangles, sewn
on with black silk. The
open hem is made by
drawing out threads
horizontally and verti-
cally (see No. 199). No.
200 shows how a gold sou-
tache is threaded through
the spaces left by drawing
out the threads. No. 201
shows the point de reprise
stitches of grey silk which
make the star patterns
with the soutache. The
threads are then drawn out horizontally to form the fringe and
the cover is laid between damp cloths and ironed.

Nos. 202, 203, & 205. Antimacassar (Point Russe Crochet). Square of écru-coloured guipure gauze 17 inches in diameter, with 9 inches left plain in the centre. For the open-worked pattern draw out 14 threads, and work every 8 of the threads left untouched with one buttonhole stitch of écru-coloured thread. A wheel is worked in each corner. The embroidery

198.—Afternoon Tea-Cloth.

on the ground is worked from Illustration 202, with 3 shades of olive silk in point russe, chain, and cross stitch. Hem the square and add a lace border.

Nos. 204, 206, and 207. Antimacassar (Cross Stitch and Punto Tirato). Two strips of white linen gauze, 5 inches wide and 10 long, worked in punto tirato, and edged on either side by strips of écru-coloured linen gauze $1\frac{1}{2}$

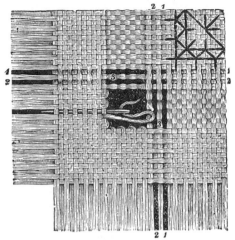

199.—DETAIL OF 198.

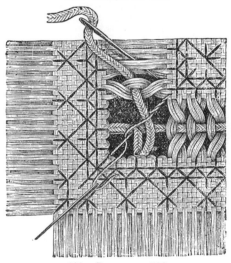

200.—DETAIL OF 198.

inch wide, worked in cross stitch.   A band of similar embroidery

201.—Detail of 198.

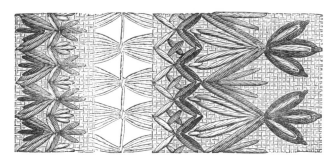

202.—Deta l of 203.

and an edging of white Russian lace is sewn round the outside

203.—ANTIMACASSAR.

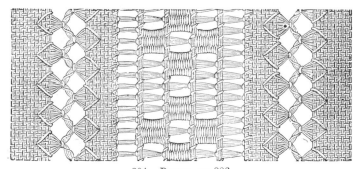

204.—DETAIL OF 206.

of the antimacassar. For the punto-tirato draw out 10 threads
on each side of the centre 50, overcast 8 of the loose threads
with white embroidery cotton, * wind the working thread round
the last 4 of the 8 threads, overcast these 4 with the next 4
threads on the other side of the pattern (see No. 204, which

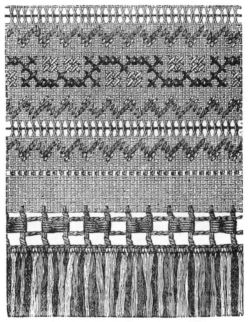

205.—DETAIL OF 203.

gives the pattern in the original size), repeat from *. Then
work over the edges of the punto tirato pattern with diagonal
stitches of écru-coloured cotton, each stitch taking in 4 threads
of the linen gauze in height. For the centre pattern leave 9
threads of the 50 on each side, and alternately draw out 4, leave
3, draw out 4, leave 9, so as to leave five spaces. To form the

bars, * overcast every 3 threads of the open rows with one stitch
of white embroidery cotton, take the needle diagonally across
the back of the 3 horizontal threads, bring the thread back
again over the front of the 3 threads according to No. 204, repeat
from *. After working the 5 rows of bars in this way, fill up

206.—ANTIMACASSAR.

207.—DETAIL OF 206.

every three bars in the centre rows with écru-coloured cotton, in
point de reprise, according to No. 204. The cross stitch on
linen gauze is worked according to No. 207, with light and dark
red silk. The antimacassar is then edged round with braid

·embroidered in the same way, and worked at the corners in
feather stitch with similar silk. The braid is sewn on to the
linen gauze with herring-bone stitches of dark red silk. The
Russian lace is then sewn round, pleated at the corners, as shown
in the illustration.

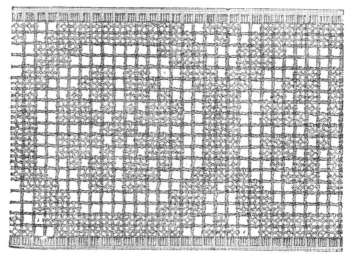

208.—BORDER FOR HANDKERCHIEFS.

No. 208. Border for Handkerchiefs. Ground of fine
cambric, with a border in punto tirato, filled in with fine stitches
of point d'esprit and buttonhole.

ORNAMENTAL NEEDLEWORK.

———◦◦———

ARTICLES FOR THE DRAWING-ROOM.

Jardinière—Footstools—Couch with Cushion—Chairs—Fire-Screen — Music-Stool—Window Lambrequin — Folio — Paper-Baskets — Lamp-Screen—Whatnot—Sofa-Cushion.

Nos. 209 and 210. Jardinière (Embroidery). Jardinière of lacquered white cane, gilded at the points. For the embroidery (see Illustration 210) vandyke the edges of a strip of black cloth, and work the rosebuds with red and green silk in satin stitch, the tendrils in point russe and overcast stitch with yellow filoselle.

No. 211. Footstool (Embroidery). Framework of black carved wood, relieved with gilding. The cushion has an embroidery worked on a ground of pale blue cloth, with bronze-coloured purse silk and filoselle. Having traced the design, fill up the leaves with double strands of coloured purse silk, sewn on with some contrasting colour. In the original, shades of bronze and maize-yellow are used.

No. 212. Foot-Rest (Embroidery). Frame of black polished wood, with cushions of black satin quilted with blue spun silk buttons. In the centre is an embroidered border worked on écru-coloured, woven with two shades of blue in a damask pattern, and worked over with split filoselle in satin stitch, overcast stitch, and point russe. The cornflowers are worked with blue silk, with brown calices; the squares are worked across with blue silk and short point russe stitches of brown at the cross-points. The border is worked to correspond, and a leaf-patterned pleating of black satin is arranged on each side of the embroidery.

209.—JARDINIÈRE.

No. 213. Couch with Sofa-Cushion and Blanket. The couch is covered with bronze-coloured rep, and the cushion is covered with holland, embroidered in blue crewel in cross stitch. The sofa-blanket has a ground of bronze cloth, lined with blue satin cloth. The outlines are then worked over in buttonhole stitch of maize purse silk, edged with gold cord. The arabesques of pale blue cloth are put on in appliqué with stitches of maize silk.

No. 214. Chair. Massive chair of walnut-wood and dark claret-coloured leather, with monograms worked with claret-coloured silk and gold thread. The antimacassar is worked on garden net with claret-coloured filoselle in cross stitch, after the pattern given in our illustration. Round the outer edge fringe of white and claret-coloured silk.

No. 215. Chair. Chair of carved polished wood, covered with blue damask, which has previously been embroidered as follows :—The flowers are outlined with several shades of pink filoselle in plain stitch, and veined in point russe. The leaves and tendrils are worked with various shades of mignonette, olive-green, and brown silk.

No. 216. Screen. Blue satin screen, embroidered with coloured silks. The framework is of black and gold bamboo cane.

No. 217. Music-Stool, of carved and polished wood, with circular cushion, covered with alternate stripes of red plush and red satin in the centre, and puffings of red plush outside. The centre stripe of satin is 5 inches wide and 40 long, and is covered with gold net and an appliqué design, cut out of old-gold satin, edged with bronze purse silk, sewn on with pale bronze sewing-silk. The appliqué designs are worked in feather and overcast stitch, and in point russe, with several shades of pink and red silk. On each side of this stripe is a braid of old-gold silk brocade, worked in filoselle. Beyond the braid is a stripe of red plush, 4 inches wide, embroidered with old-gold silk cord. Some of the pattern is filled up with red silk, carried across in a diamond pattern, and crossed with pink silk. The veining, tendrils, and knotted stitch are worked with old-gold silk. The plush and satin centre is then edged with a thick gold cord, arranged in loops at each corner, and ending in a tassel.

—Detail of 209.

211—Footstool (Embroidery).

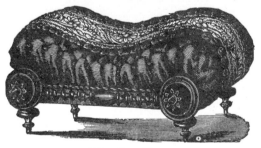

212.—Foot-Rest.

No. 218. Lambrequin for a Window. Lambrequin of dark brown cashmere, slightly wadded and lined with brown

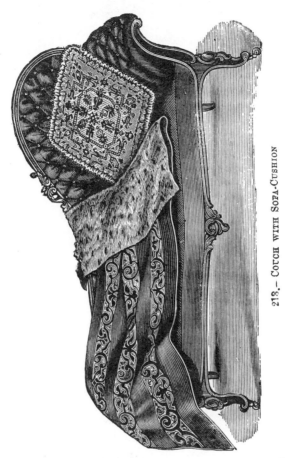

218.— Couch with Sofa-Cushion

cloth: it is then quilted with brown silk in diamond pattern. Two stripes of écru Java canvas are then embroidered with dark

wool in cross stitch, and with pale brown filoselle. On each side
of the wool-work draw out eight double threads of the canvas,
and fold back the horizontal threads so as to form a border of

214.—CHAIR.

loops. Each stripe is then edged with a tasselled fringe of brown
wool, and sewn on the lambrequin.

No. 219.   Folio for Engravings, &c. (Appliqué).   The frame
is made of polished hazelwood and fitted with a metal lock.   In

the centre is a circular appliqué embroidery. The figures are cut out of flesh-coloured cloth, the wings of white, and the emblems of brown taffetas. The veil is outlined with stitches of silver-grey silk. The musical emblems are cut out of pale

215.—Chair of Polished Wood.

blue silk, sewn on with silver filoselle. The outlines are then lined with gold cord.

No. 220. Card-Basket. Basket of black polished cane, resting on gilt feet, and having an embroidery worked on a ground of black velvet in satin overcast, and knotted stitch, and

in point russe. The poppies are worked with different shades
of red, the cornflowers with blue, the wheatears with maize silk.
The leaves and stems are embroidered partly with brown, partly
with green silk. The sewing on of the embroidery is hidden

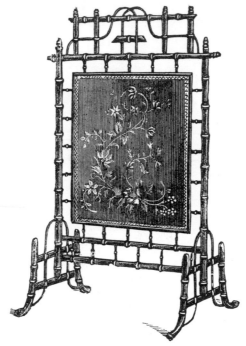

216.—Screen.

with gold cord, and between each section is a ruching of blue
silk.

Nos. 221 and 222. Waste-Paper Basket with Lambrequin.
The frame which supports the basket is made of gilt reeds, and
in each upright stem is hung a gilt ring, according to Illus-

tration No. 221. The basket itself has a lid, and is made
of lacquered black wickerwork; it is ornamented with lam-
brequins, of which No. 222 gives the full-sized pattern. The
ground is of grey cloth, with an appliqué embroidered in
satin and overcast stitch with red silks of various shades. The
ears of corn are worked in chain, and the cornflowers in satin

217.—MUSIC-STOOL.

stitch—the former with yellow filoselle and purse silk, and the
latter with blue silk. The large leaves are in appliqué of dark
green cloth, worked in overcast stitch with green silk. Light
blue for the forget-me-nots, and yellow silk for the stamens,
worked in knotted stitch; the veinings, stems, and leaves are
worked in satin and overcast stitch, with green and brown purse

silks. Round the edge of the lambrequin is a border of grey taffetas, worked with grey silk in buttonhole stitch, and ornamented with gold cord.

No. 223. Embroidered Lamp-Shade. Stand of polished black wood, with screw for raising or lowering the shade at

218.—LAMBREQUIN.

pleasure. Shade of black velvet, with deep border of peacock's feathers. Round the velvet is a border of gold soutache arranged in chain pattern. The centre embroidery is worked with gold thread in lace stitch. Arrange the spangles according to illustration.

No. 224. What-Not. Framework of bamboo and red cane, tipped with ivory studs. The stands are made of sheets of cardboard, on which are arranged dried flowers, leaves, and ferns. These are then covered with sheets of glass, and lined with silver or stamped paper.

219.—FOLIO FOR ENGRAVINGS.

No. 225. Folio for Music-Papers, &c. The cardboard sides of the folio covered with blue satin, and lined with black lutestring, are encased in a light and elegant frame of black polished cane studded with gilt knobs. In the centre is a cretonne embroidery in appliqué, and on each side of the front tassels and blue silk twisted cords are introduced.

Nos. 226, 227, and 230. Embroidered Chairs for Drawing-room Boudoir. Nos. 226 and 227. Frame of brown carved wood and cushion of brown rep, with appliqué embroidery. Illustration No. 226 gives the design for the latter; the dark figures are appliqué in brown velvet, edged with gold soutache and gold cord, and worked with chain stitch of maize-coloured silk. The rest of the embroidery is worked with two shades of brown silk in satin, overcast, and knotted stitch. The gold cord and soutache are sewn on with maize-coloured and with black silk. The back of the chair has an embroidery on a ground of brown velvet in appliqué satin and overcast stitch. The music-book is worked with an appliqué of grey taffetas, embroidered with black and grey silk. The harp and trumpet are embroidered with brown silk and gold cord in satin and overcast stitch, and appliqué of brown taffetas. The harp-strings are made of gold cord. The mandoline is embroidered with three shades of brown silk, the strings being embroidered with silver threads. The branches and tendrils are worked with different shades of brown silk in satin and overcast stitch. The sewing on of the embroidery is hidden by gold cord. No. 230. Frame of dark polished wood, with cushions of grey plush, and embroidery in Gobelin stitch.

Nos. 228 and 229. Work-Case, or "Atrappe." Both patterns may be used simply as bonbonnières and hung upon a Christmas tree. In our present pattern the case is cut out of a square of canvas and lined with gauze. The design, a small figure hold-ing a Christmas tree, is embroidered as follows:—The head of the figure is merely cut from a carte de visite photograph; the long robe is cut out of scarlet or brown cloth, and sewn on with gold-coloured silk. The long beard is worked with inter-lacing stitches of white wool, and the Christmas tree with various shades of green wool and coloured silk. The case is then folded (see Illustration No. 228), and finished off with a red worsted cord and tassels.

Nos. 231 to 233. Sofa-Cushion (Embroidery). Square

cushion, worked partly on yellow satin, partly on coarse canvas. The canvas squares are embroidered from Illustration No. 233 in Smyrna stitch, with coral filoselle, with dark red balls of wool. These balls are made with a thirtyfold strand of red wool, tied at intervals with red silk, and cut between the tying. The satin squares are stretched on cardboard, and embroidered from the design given in Illustration No. 232. The cornflowers are worked with pale blue filoselle, the calices with olive green and yellow in chain and satin stitch. The blossoms are embroidered with coral, and the tendrils with olive green in overcast stitch. The cover is then sewn on to the cushion, which is edged with thick red silk cord, ornamented with balls of wool. The cushion has also a handle of wood, covered with dark red wool, and threaded with a silk cord.

Nos. 234 to 236. Folio-Stand. Framework of polished wood, delicately carved and studded with gold. In the centre is an oval of red velvet, on which is an embroidery of cretonne appliqué sewn on with filoselle of the same colours. Gold cantille and gold thread are also used in the embroidery. Illustrations Nos. 235 and 236 give the design in the original size.

Nos. 237 and 238. Case for Letters, Papers, &c. Square case of black polished cane, studded with silver knobs, and lined with white glazed paper. Inside are partitions for paper, envelopes, &c. Folds of lilac silk are inserted along the sides. On the lid is an appliqué design. It is embroidered on a vandyked square of white cloth in knotted and feather stitch, with lilac and shaded green silk.

No. 239. Sofa-Cushion with Cover in Point Lace. Circular cushion arranged in scalloped puffings, covered with blue grosgrain silk and fitted in the centre with an embroidery of point lace. The puffings are drawn up out of a strip of blue silk, and a vandyked ruching of the same material hides their sewing on. The cover, of which we give a section, is worked as follows:—

Trace the design on tracing-paper, and sew a narrow white silk

220.—CARD-BASKET.

221.—WASTE-PAPER BASKET.

braid over the outlines. The Venetian bars and lace stitches

222.—DETAIL OF 221.

are embroidered with white purse silk.   Blue silk cord and gold

223.—Embroidered Lamp-Shade.

208

cord are then sewn along the centre of the braid, and the outer edge of the embroidery is finished off with purls of white silk.

No. 240. Ornamental Footstool (Embroidery). Circular cushion of red cloth, with vandykes of the same material. Between the latter a fur border, sewed on dark blue flannel, is

224.—WHAT-NOT.

introduced. The vandykes are scalloped round the edges, and sewed on to the circle, which is lined with grey flannel, and the embroidery worked as follows :—The smaller star-shaped figures are cut out of white cloth, and sewed on in point russe and knotted stitch with red silk. The gold soutache is sewed on with red silk, and the cross seams worked with green and yellow silks alternately. The triangles of grey cloth are sewed on in chain stitch and point russe, partly with red and white, partly with green and white silks. The two lines round the circle are worked in interlacing buttonhole stitch with green silk. The lower part of the cushion is covered with leather, and the seam hidden by a thick worsted cord.

Nos. 241 and 242. Waste-Paper Basket in polished cane, with crystal beads. The four sides are cut out of cardboard,

225.—Folio for Music-Papers, &c.

lined with wadding and blue silk quilted in diamonds. Outside the cardboard is covered with plaited straw, embroidered as follows:—The stile is worked in plain and interlacing satin stitch with several shades of brown silk, the bird with blue, and the reeds and sprays with brown and green silk. A blue silk cord is then arranged round each section of the tray, as shown in the illustration.

No. 243. Ornamental Work-Bag. Bag of striped red and white silk, ornamented with gold-coloured and blue silk braid.

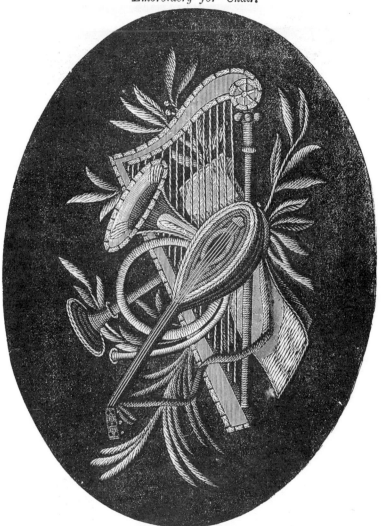

226.—DETAIL OF 227.

227.—Chair.

228.—Work-Case.

229.—Detail of 228.

230.—Another Chair.

The bag is lined with white gauze and white cashmere. The white stripes are embroidered alternately with blue braid sewed on with chain stitches of white silk, and gold braid sewed on with herring-boning of green or black silk. The red stripes are embroidered with white and yellow silk in feather-stitch and

231.—SOFA-CUSHION.

point russe. Between the embroidery and the pleated sides of blue satin is a ruching of blue satin ribbon. Cord and button of blue silk.

No. 244. Work-Stand (Embroidery). On a stand of gilt bronze a small oblong folio is placed, the sheets of which contain all necessary requisites for work. The sheets or tablets are movable, and made of cardboard set in a narrow frame.

232.—DETAIL OF 231.

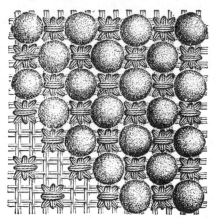

233.—DETAIL OF 231.

They are covered with blue satin, along which are several embroidered straps to hold the scissors, bodkin, stiletto, &c.

The straps are of white cloth, embroidered with yellow silk and gold cord. The needle-book has vandyked leaves of white flannel, and on the outside is ornamented with a monogram of gold thread worked in satin and overcast stitch. A narrow

234.—Folio-Stand.

blue satin ribbon is threaded through the reels of cotton, and a small bag is arranged as shown in our illustration.

Nos. 245 to 247. Chair of dark polished wood, upholstered with red-brown velvet, and embroidered on the seat and back. Round the seat is a heavy fringe and tassels. A section of the border is represented in No. 245. For the double lines which edge the border sew on two threads of fawn-coloured filoselle in 2 shades, with overcast stitches of the same coloured sewing-silk, and fill up the spaces between the inner double lines in point russe, with olive silk of 2 shapes, and in the outer double lines with cream and reseda silk in point russe. The diagonal double lines in No. 245 sew on reseda silk

235.—DETAIL OF 234.

with the same colour, and fill up with silk of a paler shade in point russe. The leaves are worked in slanting buttonhole stitch, with red and yellow silk. No. 246 gives a section of the border: the diamond pattern is outlined with reseda filoselle, the hollows with pink, and the rosettes in slanting buttonhole and knotted stitch, with peacock and yellow silk. The cross patterns between are worked with pale blue filoselle sewn with peacock silk. In the centre part, the corner figure is worked in diagonal buttonhole stitch with peacock silk. This pattern is continued with 3 shades of bronze filoselle, sewn on with silk of the same colour and with knotted stitches of pale pink silk. The vandykes at the side are worked with pink silk, and the tendrils with reseda and olive; the rest of the embroidery being put in with peacock blue.

236.—DETAIL OF 234.

Nos. 248 and 249. Etruscan Stool. Walnut-wood stool, upholstered with velvet, and having a centre stripe of embroidery. The design for the latter is worked from No. 249, in cross stitch, with wool and filoselle, the colours used being three shades of yellow-green, three shades olive, four shades red, and four shades blue. The embroidery is then finished off by a twisted silk cord. Similar cord and fringe of suitable colour round the velvet.

217

ARTICLES FOR THE STUDY AND SMOKING-ROOM.

Lamp-Mat and Shade—Jardinière—Tray for Writing-Table—Cigar-Table—
Match-Case—Cigar Ash-Trays—Lamp-Screen—Chair-Bolster.

No. 250. Ornamental Lamp-Mat and Shade. These are made
of cardboard covered with green satin, with an appliqué of
green velvet fastened down with green silk in point russe. The

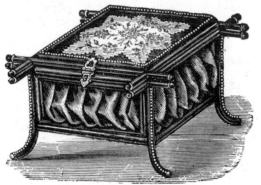

237.—CASE FOR LETTERS, PAPERS, &c. (Closed.)

mat is then ornamented with a narrow white batiste braid
with loops on each side, embroidered in feather stitch with green
silk, and arranged with bands of green satin in alternate stripes.
The wrong side of the mat is lined with green oilcloth, sewn on
with buttonhole stitch. When the pattern for the shade has
been cut out, covered with satin and sewn together, 6 strips of
cardboard are cut out, 1 inch by 6 inches, covered with satin,
and sewn on at regular intervals. For each section cut out an
appliqué of green Florence silk and crape, and sew it on. Work the

218

edge in buttonhole stitch, and the rest in chain and point russe. Pleat it into the top, and ornament the latter to correspond with the mat.

No. 251. Jardinière (Embroidery). The sexagonal flower-tray rests on a stand of bamboo cane, and is ornamented with an embroidery. On a ground of blue cloth work the corner-pieces and stars with an appliqué of maize and yellow cloth, edged with blue soutache, the cornflowers with red and blue,

238.—Case for Letters, Papers, &c. (Open.)

the stems and calices with green silk in chain stitch. The embroidery may be replaced by majolica tablets.

No. 252. Tray for Writing Materials (Embroidery). Shallow tray of bronze covered with leather, and lined with brown velvet. A border of golden stitch worked on canvas with black and white filoselle, and gold soutache is introduced round the tray.

Nos. 253 to 255. Cigar-Table (Embroidery). Table of carved brown wood. The polished surface is carved in relief. It is intended to hold a cigar-tray with matches, a lamp-stand, an ash-tray and cigar-cutter, which are all made *en suite* of the same

239.—SOFA-CUSHION.

carved wood. Round the table are strips of embroidery form-ing a fringe and ending in tassels. They are cut out of red, yellow, blue, and black cloth, and are vandyked round the edges. The embroidery of the design given in Illustration 253 is worked in chain stitch, knotted stitch, and point russe with coloured silks. No. 254 represents an appliqué of white cloth with buttonhole stitches of red, feather stitch of shaded green, and point russe embroidery of black and yellow silks. The sewing on of the strips is hidden by strong worsted cord, and the colour of the tassels should correspond with the prevailing colour of the embroidery.

Nos. 256 and 259. Case for Lucifer-Matches. The case is made of wood, lined with morocco, and ornamented with a

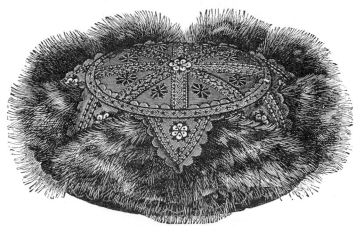

240.—Ornamental Footstool.

border of beadwork in the following colours:—Black, steel, crystal, milk-white, and pale blue. See Illustration 258.

Nos. 257 and 260. Tray for Cigar-Ash. Tray of gold bronze, with lambrequin of blue taffetas, of which the pattern is given in Illustration 260. The appliqué design is cut out of brown perforated cardboard, and sewn on with brown and gold-coloured silk. There is also a feather stitching of green, and chain stitching of blue filoselle. The grelots are of blue spun silk.

Nos. 258 and 261. Tray for Cigar-Ash. Porcelain tray on a

wooden stand, with border of cross stitch. See Illustration 261. The colours required are gold, crystal, and milk-white beads, claret-coloured and navy-blue silk.

No. 262. Lamp-Screen of Cardboard and Silk. This screen consists of a carved wooden stand, on which is fixed a circular piece of cardboard covered with green silk and edged with lace. Cut a round piece of cardboard $7\frac{1}{2}$ inches in diameter, trace upon it the designs seen in the illustrations; pierce the small holes with a large needle and cut out the figures with a sharp knife. Then cover the cardboard on both sides with green silk,

241.—Waste Paper Basket.

turn in the edges, and overcast them together all round. Sew on a black lace edging 1 inch deep, and over that a white lace edging $\frac{1}{2}$-inch deep, set on full. Cover the stitches with a gold border, and fix the screen to the stand.

Nos. 263 and 264. Neck-Rest (Cross Stitch). The centre part of the cover for this cushion is made of écru-coloured Aida cloth, embroidered with filoselle, from the pattern given in No. 264. The colours used are 3 shades of olive-green and 3 of red. The cushion is covered at each end with olive green plush, and finished with thick silk cord and chenille tassels.

ARTICLES FOR THE BEDROOM.

Bracket — Puff-Box — Hand-Glass — Pin-Box — Toilet-Box — Clothes-Bag — Brush and Comb Case—Toilet-Cushion—Towel—Towel-Stand —Glove-Case—Lamp-Mat—Footstool—Toilet-Cushion—Basket for Washed Laces.

No. 265. Bracket for Bedroom. This basket of brown polished cane is intended to be fastened to the wall, and is fitted

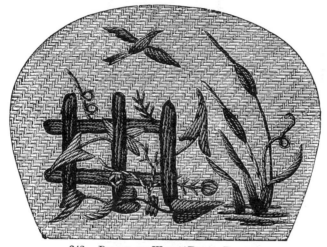

242.—Detail of Waste-Paper Basket.

with a piece of cardboard covered with flutings of peacock-blue silk, edged with straw braid at the top. A square pincushion of peacock silk, edged with blue silk cord. Bows of blue satin ribbon are sewn on each side of the pleats. The front of the basket has a trimming of balls of peacock silk, and a diamond-shaped piece of blue satin embroidered in chain stitch and point russe with different shades of peacock-blue silk.

223

No. 266. Puff-Box. Puff Powder-Box, with cushion covered with olive-green velvet, buttoned down with small buttons covered with the same material. Below the cushion double vandyked borders with tassels of coloured wool and silk.

243.—ORNAMENTAL WORK-BAG.

No. 267. Hand-Glass (Cretonne Embroidery). The wooden frame of the glass is covered with black satin, which has an appliqué embroidery of cretonne, cut out and arranged according to taste, and sewn on with purse silk of different colours.

No. 268. Pin-Box. Circular pin-box of cardboard, covered

with black cashmere, lined with blue satin, and embroidered outside with two shades of brown and green silk in point russe. The narrow rim and handles of the box are made of bronze.

Nos. 269 and 269a. Toilet-Box (Open and Shut). Wicker basket covered with brown cashmere, and fitted with a lambre-

244.—WORK-STAND.

quin of white transparent material, which is vandyked and bound with brown braid. Above the braid is an embroidery of brown silk in point russe, and below it is a fringe of brown woollen balls. The sewing on of the lambrequin is hidden by a ruching of box-pleated brown braid. The basket is lined with the same material as that used for the lambrequin, and

245.—DETAIL OF 247.

246.—DETAIL OF 247.

is fitted with four pockets with embroidered flaps. Each flap has two rows of pale brown vandyked braid with a herring-

247.—Chair with Embroidery.

248.—Etruscan Stool.

boning of brown silk. The star patterns are embroidered in

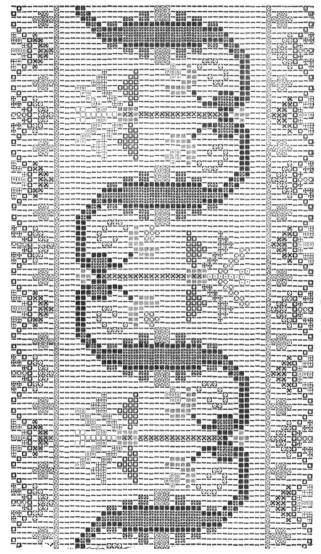

249.—DETAIL OF 248.

point russe with pale brown silk, sewn on with dark brown purse silk, and have in the centre a Smyrna stitch of pale brown. The outlines are then gone over with brown soutache. At the bottom of the basket is a piece of cardboard covered with the same material as the lining, and fitted with straps of brown worsted braid, to hold brushes, combs, &c. This tray has also an embroidery of pale yellow filoselle worked in chain stitch on brown braid. The covering of the lid has an embroidery of brown and maize-coloured purse-silk in chain stitch and point russe. Round the outer edge is a box-pleating of brown braid and bows of ribbon.

Nos. 270 and 270A. Window-Screen. Oblong screen of polished cane filled with linen gauze embroidered in alternate stripes of cross and double satin stitch. (For the network pattern see No. 270.) It is worked with 8 rows of cross-stitch, each stitch taking in 2 threads of the linen, while 4 threads are left between each row. Then work across the stripe rows of 22 cross-stitches, and draw out the threads as shown in No. 270A. A point lace braid is sewn between the stripes and closely worked over with buttonhole stitches. The same illustration gives clearly the pattern for the close stripe. The linen is hemmed round with an open hem, and sewn into the frame with white silk cord.

No. 271. Brush and Comb Case. Case of cardboard, covered with olive-green leather, and lined with pressed paper. The design for the embroidery is worked on silver moirée antique, in chain, knotted, and feather stitch. The cornflowers are embroidered with blue, the forget-me-nots with pale pink, and the leaves with green silk. The wheatears are embroidered with gold thread.

No. 272. Toilet-Cushion (Embroidery). Low circular cushion, covered with pink satin, and having a centre embroidery worked on white cloth, vandyked at the edges. The outer edge is arranged in puffings, with straps of white cloth as shown

250.—ORNAMENTAL LAMP-MAT AND SHADE.

251.—JARDINIÈRE.

in illustration. Trace the embroidery design, and work the lace stitches of the corner pieces with fine white silk. The rose-buds and the may-blossoms are embroidered in chain stitch with split filoselle of the natural colours; the foliage in over-cast and feather-stitch with shaded green silk. A ruching of pink satin encircles the embroidery. (See illustration.)

Nos. 273 to 276. Towel Embroidered in Cord Stitch. This stitch is easily worked, and in many styles of embroidery produces a better effect than satin stitch. The cloths to be embroidered must be selected with a smooth stripe, woven at each

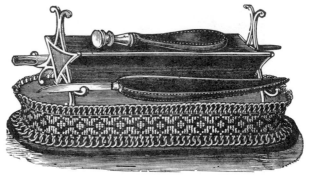

252.—TRAY FOR WRITING MATERIALS.

end of the rough centre. The design is traced on this stripe, and the embroidery is worked with red cotton, according to our illustrations 274 and 276. The last illustration, 276, shows the overcast stitch which produces the cord-like effect from which the stitch receives its name. The fringe is then made with two rows of double knots. The monogram is worked on the wrong side of the cloth. The corded stitch is worked in 4 rows, the fourth being like the third (Illustration 276), but worked from the wrong side.

Nos. 277 to 280. Towel-Stand. Stand of black polished

wood. The towels are fringed, and have an embroidery in cross
stitch, of which the patterns are given in Illustrations 278 and
280. The upper towel is embroidered in Jacquard stitch according to the pattern given in 279 and 280. The threads are
drawn out when the work is completed. For No. 280 the colours
required are dark red, light red, blue, green, yellow. For

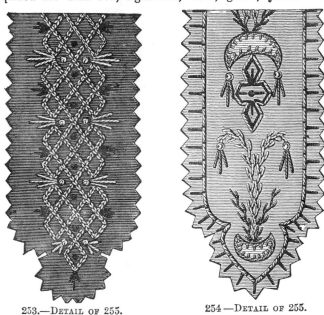

253.—Detail of 255.　　　　254.—Detail of 255.

No. 278, dark red, light red, black, yellow, green, dark blue
light blue. For No. 279, blue, red.

　　Nos. 281 and 283. Glove-Case (Appliqué). The case is cut
out of one piece of marone velvet and two pieces of white satin,
each 12 by 6 inches. The velvet which forms the outside of the
case has an appliqué design (see Illustration 283) worked on a
ground of white cloth, vandyked round the edge. The flowers

are embroidered in chain stitch with coral silk of several shades,
the stamina with yellow silk in knotted stitch and point russe,

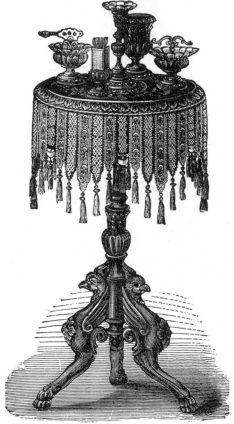

255.—CIGAR TABLE. (Embroidery.)

the tendrils with olive silks in feather stitch, the buds in knotted
stitch with pink silk. A ruching of olive satin ribbon is arranged
round the appliqué, and of marone satin round the outer edge.

234

The appliqué is sewed on with gold thread in chain stitch. The velvet is then wadded and lined with satin, and the upper and lower parts are tied together with olive and marone satin ribbon.

Nos. 282 and 284. Lamp-Mat (Point Russe). Circular

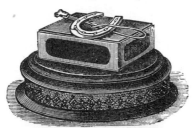

256.—Case for Lucifer-Matches.

257.—Tray for Cigar-Ash.

mat of cardboard 9 or 10 inches in diameter, and covered with blue satin. Round the centre are three rows of fancy straw and a border in which folded leaves of blue satin are arranged alternately with leaves of white cloth. The latter (see Illustration 284) are vandyked, and embroidered with blue silk.

Nos. 285, 286, 287, and 288. Basket, &c., for Washed Laces, Rough-Dried Linen, &c. Oblong willow basket with a lid, lined with grey leather, and ornamented outside with pockets of blue linen. Illustration 288 gives the pattern for the embroidery of the strips. It is worked with blue and red cotton in point russe, Tassels of red and blue are arranged at the

258.—TRAY FOR CIGAR-ASH.

259.—DETAIL OF 256.

ends of the straps. The lining is fastened to the basket with small metal studs. Illustration 286 shows an ironing blanket of white frieze, crocheted round with blue and red cotton. The border is worked in Holbein stitch, and so appears exactly alike on each side (see Illustration 287).

Nos. 290 and 291. Curtain-Band (Crochet). Begin in the centre of the close pattern, which is worked in two halves with 16 stitches. 1st row: Miss 1, 7 double, 3 double in next stitch, 7 double. 2nd row: 1 chain, miss 1, 7 double (always in back part of stitch), 3 double in next stitch, 7 double; repeat this row 80 times, but at the end of the 16 and 17, 30,

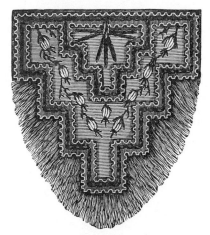

260.—DETAIL OF 257.

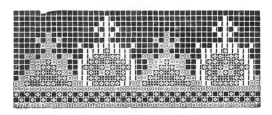

261.—DETAIL OF 258.

31, 46, 47, 60, 61, 72, and 73 decrease 1, and at the beginning of each of these rows miss 2 instead of 1. The other half is crocheted in the same way, joining together in the centre crochet as follows:—8 purl of 5 chain and 1 double, joining centre of

237

2nd purl to one side of the opening. Between the close

262.—LAMP-SCREEN OF CARDBOARD AND SILK.
238

patterns crochet 1st row : 6 chain, 1 purl, 5 chain, join to marginal stitch, * going back along the 5 chain, 4 double, 1 slip stitch, 1 purl, 4 chain, 1 purl, 5 chain, join to marginal stitch ; repeat from * 32 times, at the last repetition instead of 1

263.—CHAIR BOLSTER.

264.—DETAIL OF 263.

purl, 5 chain, crochet 2 chain.   2nd row : Going back along the stitches, miss 1, 5 double in 5 chain, 1 slip stitch in next double of purl, *, 1 purl, 6 chain for a bar, going back along the chain, miss 1, 4 double, 1 slip stitch, 1 purl, 1 double in double of next purl, 4 double in 4 chain ; repeat from *, last of all 6 double in 6 chain. Fasten and cut the thread. 3rd row:

265.—Bracket for Bedroom.

266.—Puff-Box.

6 chain, 1 purl, join to 6th chain of bar, * 1 purl, 4 chain, 1 purl, join to next bar; repeat from * at last 6 instead of 4 chain. 4th row: Going back along these slip stitches and taking up the 2 close strips. Like 2nd row, but joining the 6th chain of the bars as shown in illustration. At each end this open-worked

267.—HAND-GLASS.

part is joined to a close part as follows:—Join to centre of close stripe, 1 slip stitch, 5 chain, 2 slip stitch in end of bar at the narrow end of the open-worked strip, 4 chain, 2 slip stitch in next bar, 5 chain, 2 slip stitch in 2nd and 3rd of 5 double of close strip. Turn the work, along preceding stitches 1 chain, miss **1, 20** double, * turn the work, along preceding stitches 1 chain, miss 1, 1 double before every double except the first; repeat from * 4 times, diminishing, of course, the number of stitches and working always in back part of stitch. Then round the outer edge 1 round as follows :—1 treble in margin, twice alternately 2 chain, 1 treble, 3 purl, 1 treble in last treble; repeat from *. For the loops crochet 3 rows in a ribbed pattern along foundation chains of 110 stitches.

ARTICLES FOR PERSONAL ADORNMENT.

Fichu—Cravats—Child's Collar—Fan—Chatelaines—Smoking-Cap—Hunting-Pouch.

291. Fichu of White Crêpe de Chine. Triangular piece of white crêpe de chine, measuring fifteen inches along the straight edge. Border of same material embroidered in chain stitch.

268.—PIN-BOX.

The roses are worked with pink, the stamens with yellow, the leaves and tendrils with shaded green silks. Care must be taken to embroider the border on the wrong side of that part of the fichu which is turned back *en revers*. Round the edge a knotted fringe of white floss silk.

Nos. 292 and 293. Cravatte with Corded Ribbon and Embroidery. The ribbon should measure 62 inches long, and is embroidered at each end with white purse silk. No. 294 shows the pattern of the embroidery, which is worked on fine mull muslin. The ground is cut away as usual from beneath the wheels.

Nos. 294 and 297. Collar for Children (Crochet). For the

guipure-like pattern proceed as follows:—9 chain, 1 purl of 5 chain and 1 double; repeat as often as necessary; this forms the foundation. 1st row: 18 chain, 1 double in 3rd stitch, * 1 chain, 1 purl, 7 chain, miss 1 purl, 1 double in 3rd stitch before next purl, 7 chain, join to last double but one, 1 slip stitch, 1 double 9 treble, 1 double, 1 slip stitch in 7 chain, join to next stitch, 1 chain, 1 purl, 7 chain, miss 1 purl, 1 double in 3rd stitch before next purl; repeat from *, at the end of the row 1 chain, 1 purl,

269.—Toilet-Box.

2 chain, 1 double long treble in 1st stitch. 2nd row: 9 chain, * miss 1 purl, 1 double in 3rd stitch before next purl, 1 chain, 1 purl, 1 chain, 7 treble with 1 chain between each in centre 7 treble of 9 treble, 3 chain, 1 double in 3rd stitch before next purl, 1 chain, 1 purl, 7 chain, repeat from * at last in 3rd chain after last double. 3rd row: 11 chain, * 1 double in 3rd chain before next purl, 1 chain, 1 purl, 7 chain, 1 double in chain between 1st and 2nd of 7 treble, 1 chain, 1 purl, 7 chain, 1 double in chain before the last of the 7 treble, chain, 1 purl, 7 chain; repeat from *. 1 double in centre of

1

7 chain; repeat now 1st to 3rd rows, letting the pattern occur in reversed position (see Illustration 417). Round the outer edge of the collar proceed as follows:—1st round: 1 treble, 3 chain; repeat. Round the neck 4 chain instead of 3. 2nd row (lower edge): * 4 times alternately 3 double in 3 chain, 1 double in treble, then 7 chain, join to 10th of 16 double, 7 chain, join to 4th of same 16 chain, going back along the last stitches 5 double with 1 purl between the two last, in the first 4 of the next 7 chain, 2 chain, 3 purl, 2 chain, 5 double, with 1 purl

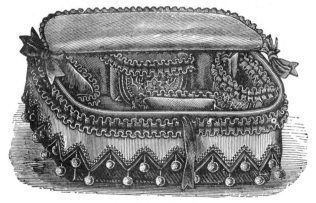

269ᴀ.—Toilet-Box Open.

between the 2 first in last 4 of 7 chain, 1 slip stitch in last of 16 double; repeat from *. Round the neck crochet 5 double in 4 chain, and 1 double in each treble; the two front ends of this collar are crocheted separately as far as the centre of the back of the neck, and then it is joined in a whole.

Nos. 295 and 296. Necktie. Necktie of ivory-coloured corded ribbon, embroidered with silk of the same colour, the embroidery being worked after the design given in No. 294.

No. 298. Fan for Evening Dress (Point Lace). Ivory frame,

delicately carved, and made up with an embroidery on white batiste. White silk cord and tassels complete the fan. The

270.—WINDOW-SCREEN.

embroidery is worked with point-lace braid, satin stitch, button-hole stitch with purls, and Venetian bars. Round the outer margin is a narrow pearl edging. The ground is cut away as shown in the illustration.

No. 299. Chatelaine Pocket. Bag of brown velvet lined with white silk, suspended by a cord of brown silk passementerie worked in cross stitch with white silk, and ornamented with brown silk buttons and tassels. The front of the pocket has an embroidery of point lace, for which we give the design in

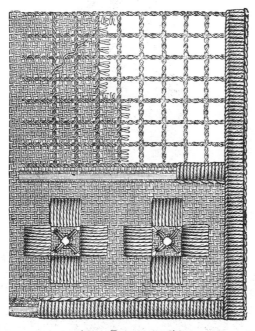

270A.—DETAIL OF 270.

Illustration 302. Trace the design on tracing paper with a white silk braid, and work the bars and various lace stitches with white purse silk. The scallops round the outer edge are worked with buttonhole stitches over loops of white silk, the purls being put in according to illustration.

No. 300. Aumônière. This is of pale blue silk, drawn up

with cords of the same shade. The lower part consists of an

271.—BRUSH AND COMB-BAG.

272.—TOILET-CUSHION.

embroidery design in white purse silk. Trace the design on
paper and embroider it over muslin in satin, knotted, and

buttonhole stitches. The bag is fitted with silver chains and
medallion to fix it to the belt.

273.—Towel Embroidered in Cord-Stitch.

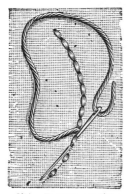

274.—Detail of 273.

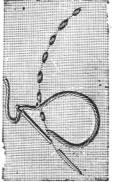

275.—Detail of 273.

Nos. 301 and 302. Glove-Case. The upper side of the case
is made of claret-coloured and of white satin ribbon, plaited
together in squares, and embroidered with silver thread and

claret-coloured silk in point russe, according to Illustration 300.

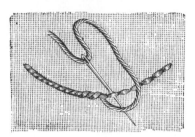

276.—DETAIL OF 273.

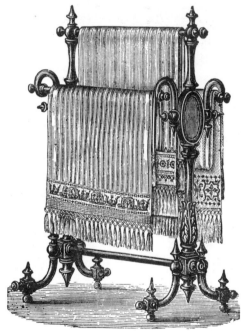

277.—TOWEL-STAND, WITH EMBROIDERED TOWELS.

250

The lower side is made of claret-coloured satin, lined with

278.—DETAIL OF 277.

279.—DETAIL OF 277.

280.—DETAIL OF 277.

281.—GLOVE-CASE.

282.—LAMP-MAT.

283.—DETAIL OF 281.

284.—DETAIL OF 282.

white, and both sides are slightly wadded with scented wadding. Round the upper edge is a box-pleated ruching of claret-coloured satin ribbon under loops of white satin ribbon. At each corner is a bow of the two colours.

Nos. 303 and 304. Smoking-Cap (Greek Pattern). Cap of brown velvet lined with leather. Stretch the velvet in an embroidery frame, and go over the design with gold and silver

285.—Basket for Washed Laces.

cord. The spangles are sewn on with yellow or white silk to match the colour.

No. 305. Hunting-Pouch. The pouch is made of leather and fitted with straps and a carbineer's hook. In front is a purse of knotted work, for which proceed as follows :—Knot 40 strands on to the foundation thread and work 25 rows in double knots, reversing the position, leaving as many strands unnoticed

as the pattern requires. To the first row of double knots add
50 strands at one side, and proceed as follows:—13 rows in
double knots in reversed position; 14th and 15th rows: with
the 11th to the 42nd strand and the 58th to the 90th, 2 double
knots; 16th to 21st rows, like preceding; 22nd to 26th rows
with all the strands single double knots, the intervals being
filled up with Josephine knots; the 25th and 26th rows form
the centre of the work, and the position of the rows must now
be reversed. The fringe is then knotted in double knots, and
the strands cut even.

286.—DETAIL OF 285.

MISCELLANEOUS ARTICLES.

Window-Curtains — Footstool and Cushions —Workstaud —Watch-Case—
Thimble-Case — Ring-Tray—Garden-Basket — Key-Bracket—Coverlet—
Garden-Furniture.

Nos. 306 and 308. Window-Blind. (Netting and Point Russe.)
Blind of fawn-coloured felt, 53 inches wide and 42 high. Five
vertical stripes of red felt, embroidered in crewels, are arranged

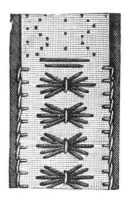

287.—Detail of 286.　　　288.—Detail of 285.

on the fawn ground at intervals. Each stripe of the red felt is
6 inches wide by 33 high, and at the lower edge they are cut
out in a square tab, as shown in our illustration. The embroidery is worked with coloured wools in chain, overcast,
feather, and satin stitch, and in point russe. On each side of
the embroidered stripes is a stripe of netting, worked with red
wool over a mesh not quite an inch wide. Each netted stripe is
5 stitches wide, and besides the 6 long stripes there are 5 short

ones to fill up the tabs cut out of the embroidered stripes. The shorter netted stripes are graduated to a point, and every netted stripe is finished by a short tassel of red wool.

Nos. 307—308a. Window-Curtain. The pattern is worked in stripes on a ground of écru-coloured jute canvas. The stripe

289.—Detail of 290.

for which the design is given in No. 308a is worked in cross stitch with Berlin wool of the following shades: 2 shades olive, red. The narrow stripe in 308a is worked in cross stitch and point russe with brown wool. Between the point russe stitches the colours used are claret wool and blue silk. The stripe given in No. 308 has a leaf pattern worked in cross stitch with red and black wool. At the lower edge the threads are drawn out for a fringe and tied into tassels with coloured wool. Balls of coloured wool are then added in all the shades used in the embroidery.

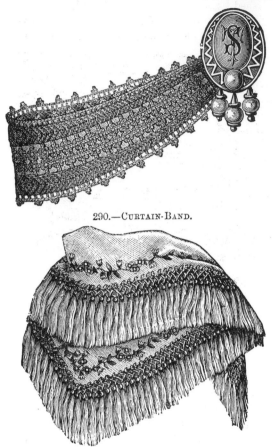

290.—Curtain-Band.

291.—Fichu.

No. 309. Cushions and Small Footstool. (Embroidery.) The framework is of polished wood and rests on four casters. The cushions are covered with black satin quilted down with **small**

292.—CRAVAT.   293.—DETAIL OF 292.

294.—CHILD'S COLLAR.

buttons and edged round with a coloured silk cord.   **The square**

cushion is also embroidered in cross stitches on a canvas ground
with Berlin wool and filoselle.   The colours used in our illustra-

295.—Detail of 296.   296.—Necktie.

297.—Detail of 294.

tion are three shades of fawn colour and pale green filoselle.   It
is finished off with a silk cord and four tassels.

Nos. 310 and 311.   Ornamental Emery Cushion.   (Knitting and Crochet.)   This pear-shaped cushion rests on a circular mat

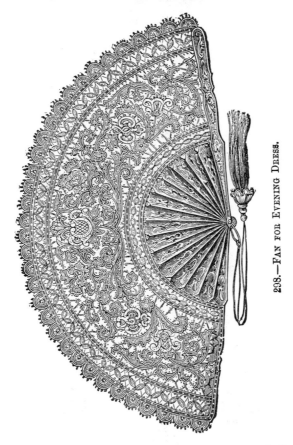

208.—FAN FOR EVENING DRESS.

covered with knitted wool, to represent the mossy bed on which the fruit might rest.   The mat measures 5 inches in diameter, and is covered with black twill.   The cushion is cut in 8 sepa-

261

rate sections, joined together and filled with emery. Then draw

299.—CHATELAINE-POCKET.

some strong thread tightly over every seam, and begin to work

300.—AUMÔNIÈRE.

the cover with green wool according to Illustration 311, which
shows clearly how the wool is worked round the cushion and

passed under every thread. Before the cover of wool is com-

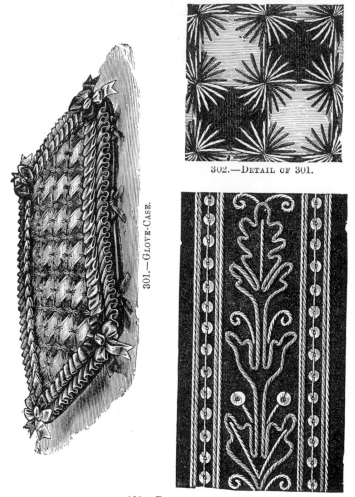

302.—DETAIL OF 301.

301.—GLOVE-CASE.

303.—DETAIL OF 304.

pleted a wire is introduced into the thin end of the pear to form
the stalk. This is wound round with green wool, and has two
leaves attached. For the latter proceed as follows : Crochet 15
chain of green wool, and then going back along them crochet

304.—SMOKING-CAP (Greek design).

305.—HUNTING-POUCH.

over fine wire 1 double, 13 treble, and for the point 1 chain ;
along the other side of the foundation chain 1 double, 13 treble,
1 double, 3 double over both ends of wire for the stem of the leaf.
The larger leaf is crocheted in a similar way along a longer

265

foundation chain. The moss is then knitted in several shades of green. Cast on 10 stitches and knit to and fro a strip of con-

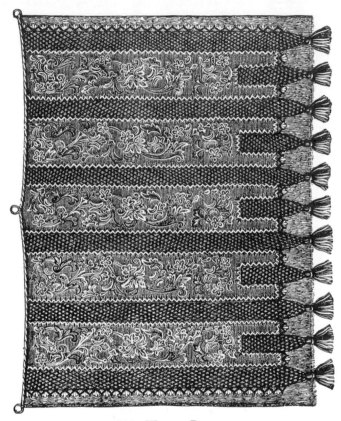

306.—WINDOW-BLIND.

siderable length. Cast off. Then damp the work and let it dry again. Cut open the stitches the narrow way of the strip and unravel them to within 2 stitches of the opposite edge. This marks the *head or border* of the moss, which is then sewn on to the mat so that each layer of moss shall hide the sewing on of the previous layer. For the star-shaped flowers proceed as

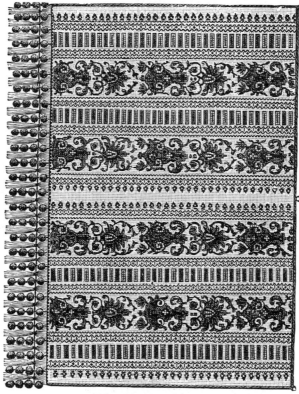

307.—WINDOW-CURTAIN.

follows: Take some yellow wool and wind it about twenty times round a mesh nearly an inch wide, pass some wire through the loops, and join the ends of the wire together. Then tie the ball

267

of wool with thread in the centre and cut the loops.   This forms

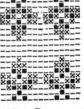

308A.— DETAIL OF
307.

308.—DETAIL OF 305.

the centre of the flower. The outside is done with white or lilac·
wool alternately. Each flower requires 24 loops round the same·
mesh ; the loops are held in place by fine wire, and fastened
round the centre ball of yellow. They are then arranged round
the cushion and sewn on to the moss.

No. 312. Work-Basket and Stand. Stand of black polished
cane with gilt rim. The basket is lined with olive-green taffetas,

309.—Cushions and Small Footstool (Embroidery).

and has in the centre of the lid a little cushion of green taffetas,
quilted and studded with small green silk buttons. Round the
cushion are vandykes of netting, embroidered with green filoselle and chenille. A ruching of green taffetas covers the
sewing on of the vandykes, and a tassel of green chenille falls
between each. Cords and tassels of olive-green silk and small
bronze chains are attached to the handle.

No. 313. Scissors-Tray and Pincushion. Circular tray of pale
grey and brown leather, scalloped round the edge with a design
of olive-green cashmere, which is sewn on to the grey leather

with blue and maize and olive-green filoselle. The centre **star** figure of cashmere is worked with blue and yellow silk and **small** buttons of blue silk. The vandykes round are embroidered **with** the same colours, and each alternate vandyke is fitted with **a** semicircular flap of pale grey, sewn on with coloured silk, **and**

310.—EMERY CUSHION.

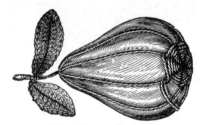

311.—DETAIL OF 310.

serving as a case for the scissors. The pincushion is wadded and covered with olive-green cashmere, crossed with blue filoselle, with centre of point russe and blue button. The cushion is edged round with buttonhole stitches of blue and yellow silk. It is sewn on with chain stitch of olive-green silk and knotted stitch of blue silk. The outer edge of the tray is worked with buttonhole stitch of olive-green silk.

No. 314. Handkerchief-Case. Case of grey twill, bound with claret-coloured braid, and embroidered with fine pearl braid of the same colour, arranged in vandykes, and sewn on with a paler shade of purse silk in knotted and overcast stitch. Two bands

312.—WORK-STAND.

of claret-coloured elastic, fitted with steel clasps, serve for the fastening.

No. 315. Case for Scent-Bottles. Pointed case of cardboard to put over the cork of scent-bottles, to prevent evaporation. It is made of four pieces of cardboard covered with red, blue, and white cloth, and sewn together with silk of the same colours. The seams are also worked with gold cord. Round the lower edge is a pleated frill of blue satin and a twisted pleat of blue

313.—Scissor-Tray.

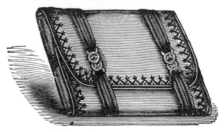

314.—Handkerchief-Case.

silk cord. Bronze droppers are sewn on, as shown in our illustration.

No. 316.   Work-Bag.   (Embroidery.)   The lower part of the

315.—Scent-Bottle Case.

316.—Work-Bag.

317.—Watch-Case.

work-case is cut out of grey twill bound with red leather, and embroidered with a design in satin and overcast stitch of bright-coloured silk. The bag is made of dark red satin, with cord and tassels of the same colour.

No. 317. Watch-Case. Case of polished cane lined with blue

318.—TRAVELLING-CUSHION (Front).

velvet wadded to hold watch. In front is a medallion of blue velvet, embroidered in satin and overcast stitch with pale blue silk.

Nos. 318 to 320. Travelling Cushion. (Embroidery.)— Circular cushion, 15 inches in diameter, filled with eider-down, and covered with an écru-coloured linen material, woven in a small check pattern. The front of the cushion is embroidered

274

in **Smyrna** stitch from the design given in No. 318, one stitch being worked in the centre of each diamond. The colours used are dark brown embroidery cotton for the diagonal lines; for the stitches in the centre of the diamonds, two paler shades of the same colour. The other side of the cushion is arranged as a pocket (see No. 319), the material being cut so as to allow of

319.—Travelling-Cushion (Back).

a **narrow** hem, and the pocket fastened with buttons and buttonholes, worked on the upper part of the cushion. For the lace, écru-coloured braid, with loops on each side, is used (see No. 320), and three shades of brown embroidery cotton. Along one side of the braid crochet as follows :—1st row, with dark brown : 3 treble drawn up together in the first three loops of the braid,

7 chain, repeat. 2nd row, with medium brown: 6 treble in the
7 chain, 1 chain, repeat. On the other side of the braid. 3rd
row, with dark brown: 1 double in first loop, 3 chain, repeat.
4th row, with medium brown: 1 double in the first chain
scallop, 5 chain, repeat. The two sides of the cushion are now

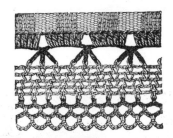

320.—Detail of 318.

321.—Blotting Roller (Embroidery).

sewn together, and a narrow brown silk braid is run through
the first row of the lace. The handle is a strip of the linen
material, $2\frac{1}{2}$ inches wide and 17 inches long, worked in Smyrna
stitch with three shades of brown embroidery cotton, and lined
with the material.

No. 321. Blotting Roller. (Embroidery.) The rollers, which are wound round with several thicknesses of good blotting paper, are moved by a handle passing through the wooden plate. The latter is covered on the under side with black glazed paper, and on the upper side with red embroidered cashmere. The

322.—DETAIL OF 325.   323.—THIMBLE-CASE.

324.—DETAIL OF 325.

pattern on the cashmere is worked with many coloured silks, in satin, overcast, knotted stitch, and point russe.

Nos. 322, 324, 325. Work-Basket. Shallow circular basket of fancy straw and polished cane. The inside is lined with blue corded silk embroidered in the pattern given in Illustration 324. Trace the design, and apply the flower medallions of point lace braid sewn on with buttonhole stitches of black silk. Stamina of yellow and black silk, the latter worked in knotted

325.—WORK-BASKET.

326.—COSY.

stitch. The tendrils are worked in overcast stitch and point russe. The remainder is chain stitch of black and yellow silks. The silk is then lined and sewn inside the basket, a blue silk cord hiding the stitches. Illustration 322 gives the separate flowers worked in a similar manner to those already described.

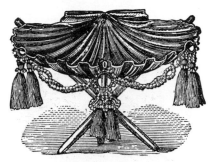

327.—Ring-Tray.

328.—Napkin-Ring.

No. 323. Thimble-Case. In the shape of a bedroom slipper. The case is covered with black leather, slightly wadded, and lined with blue satin, so that the heel may be used as a pincushion. For the embroidery of the toe see illustration. The roses and leaves are worked with shaded pink and green silks, in satin and overcast stitch.

No; 326. Cosy, Cosy of écru-coloured Baden-Baden cloth, with appliqué embroidery. The black ribbon velvet is sewn on with green filoselle in overcast stitch, and the berries are worked in satin stitch with red filoselle. The mat of fawn-coloured cloth is worked with brown and gold-coloured silk in point

329.—ORNAMENTAL PENWIPER.

330.—DETAIL OF 329.

russe. For the table, appliqué of brown velvet, with silk of the same shade. Coffee service of white cloth, sewn on with blue silk. Lining of cashmere over wadding, and at the side puffings of blue cashmere, balls and tassels of blue wool.

No. 327. Ring-Tray. Formed of a shell wound round with gold cord and cerise purse silk. A chain of steel beads threaded

on cerise purse silk is arranged as shown in illustration. The
rings are wound round with silk of the same colour and fitted
with cerise tassels.

331.—GARDEN-BASKET.

332.—BRACKET FOR KEYS.

No. 328. Dinner Napkin Ring. Of olive green leather,
perforated ready for working. In the centre is a narrow braid,

woven with coloured silks, and threaded through an opening in the ring inside which it is fastened. The embroidery is worked through the holes as follows:—The double lines in buttonhole stitch with olive silk, the spaces being filled up with a paler shade of olive in satin stitch and point russe. When the

833.—DETAIL OF 332.

embroidery is finished the ring is lined with strong cardboard, and then with green leather.

Nos. 329 and 330. Ornamental Penwiper. This novel design is shaped like a letter-box and covered with blue cloth, which has been previously embroidered in the pattern given in Illustration 330. Trace the design for the writing materials with gold and silver thread in satin, overcast, chain, and

334.—DESSERT D'OYLEYS.

buttonhole stitch, and in point russe. The envelope at the back is sewed on with overcast stitches of silver thread. On the partitions for the sides a posthorn and a ruler are embroidered with gold and silver thread, and the inside is fitted with a brush to dry the pens.

335.—Design for Coverlet.

No. 331.   Garden-Basket.   Of Japanese straw plait, threaded through with fawn-coloured braid.   At each end rosettes of braid and balls of fawn-coloured wool.   Round the upper edge **a** row of loose buttonhole stitches in fawn-coloured wool is worked, and in each stitch 9 double stitches are tatted. The basket is lined with oiled cloth, and fitted with handles of twisted Japanese straw.

336.—GARDEN-SOFA.

Nos. 332 and 333. Bracket for Keys. Bracket of dark carved wood, with narrow shelf at the top to hold any small articles, and fitted in front with hooks on which various keys are suspended.

It has also an embroidery for which the design is given in Illustration 333, and which is worked on holland with maize-coloured silk in satin and overcast stitch and in point russe.

No. 334. Dessert d'Oyleys. Serviettes of grey damask, fringed round the edge and embroidered with overcast stitch in the corners. After tracing on the damask, the outlines of the

337.—GARDEN-CHAIR.

pears, apples, plums, blackberries, the leaves, veining, and tendrils are worked with overcast stitch in scarlet marking-cotton.

No. 335. Coverlet for Cradle, &c. Coverlet of fine white flannel, edged with blue flannel. The design for the embroidery of the centre given in Illustration 335 is embroidered as follows: The cornflowers, leaves, and calices with blue silk in satin and over-

cast stitch, and the sprays with point russe and overcast stitch
with very pale blue. The lilies of the valley are embroidered
with white, and the leaves with three shades of green silk. The
border is joined to the centre with grey and blue silks in point
russe. The outer edge is scalloped, and has scallops of white
flannel at the outside ; both sets of scallops are vandyked and

338.—GARDEN-CHAIR.

worked with two shades of blue silk in chain, knotted, and
Smyrna stitch, and in point russe.

Nos. 336 to 338. Garden Furniture. These articles of furniture
are made of reeds and Japanese matting. The chair and sofa
(336 and 338) are made up with cane. The sofa-rug and neckrests on the chairs are made of linen material, woven in alter-

nate stripes of Aida and Jacquard cloth. The Aida stripe is embroidered with filoselle and crewels in the following colours: Three shades of violet, brown, olive; three shades of red; three shades of blue. The sofa-rug is lined with twill and edged with écru woollen cord the long way of the rug, and with broad fringe along the narrow ends. When the sofa-cushion and neckrests have been covered as shown in the illustration they are finished off with cord and tassels of the prevailing colours used in the embroidery, the cords and tassels being arranged in loops as shown in the various illustrations.

MACRAMÉ LACE.

MODE OF WORKING.

Introduction—Materials—Cushions—Various Stitches—Knotted Bar—Star or Diamond—Genoese Knot—Solomon's Knot—Grounding.

THIS fascinating kind of fancy-work dates as far back as the fifteenth century. The materials are inexpensive, and the lace lasts almost for ever. The work progresses rapidly, and can be made in many materials; none, however, so good as the cord made and sold for the purpose. The manipulation consists in tying knots of various kinds. This lace can be unhesitatingly recommended as a pleasant occupation and pastime.

Goethe, somewhere or other, in exalting music above every other art, does so on the ground that it produces its marvellous effects with so little display of means and tools; and if this test be applied to our present work, it will rank very high amid the rival styles of lacemaking and embroidery. No dazzling range of colours, no blending of different materials, not even a thimble and needle, are wanted to produce the charming effects of our Macramé work.

And first of all, why "Macramé?" Macramé is nothing but the name given by the Italians round about Genoa (the home and birthplace of the work) to a coarse material used for towels, the fringed ends of which are knotted in several of the lace stitches which we shall afterwards explain. As to the materials required, they are of the simplest. We advise our fair reader to begin with the coarse Macramé thread until she has learnt how to wield her weapons, and thoroughly mastered every stitch; but when that is once done, she will find herself able to work rich trimmings for black and coloured costumes both for

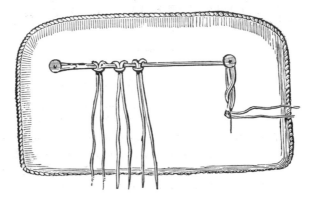

339.—Miniature Cushion, with Foundation Thread, and Putting on of the Stitches.

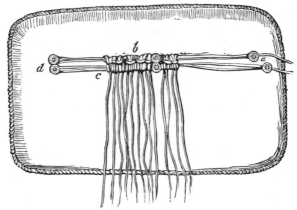

340.—First Row with a Cord.

home wear, garden parties, and seaside rambles—fairylike adornments for household and underlinen—fringes, edgings, and insertions for towels, pillows, antimacassars—covers for sofa-cushions, etc., etc. For these latter purposes she will have at

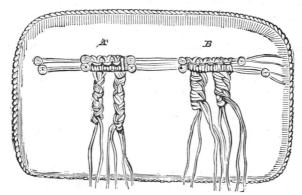

341.—Knotted Bar.   Buttonhole Knot.

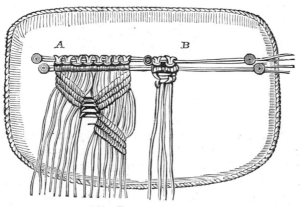

342.—Diamond or Star.

her command black, white, and coloured silks made specially for Macramé work, very fine flax thread for the white linen, brown, grey, and all shades of écru for unbleached or coloured linen and holland materials, filoselle for fancy trimmings, and so on in endless variety. But, being a beginner, she will at first try "her 'prentice hand" on the coarse Macramé thread generally preferred for trimming brackets, drawing-room tables, mantelpieces, etc.

The first thing wanted is a weighted cushion, measuring about ten inches long by seven or eight wide. The best way is to get a bag of coarse towelling of the dimensions above given, and stuff it carefully with sand and bran well mixed; the sand will give it the necessary weight, and the bran is easy to stick

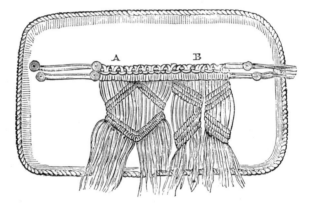

343.—Genoese Knot.   Solomon's Knot.

pins in. As to the cover of the cushion, we strongly recommend a fine dark cloth; some people advise a striped material, such as ticking, saying that the lines are a help in stretching the horizontal threads, but in our opinion the lines are often rather confusing than helpful, and we believe our pupil will find them wholly unnecessary, while cloth is much pleasanter than ticking to work upon.

The cushion made, and slightly rounded at the top, the learner will provide herself with a box of steel toilet-pins with glass heads, sold for the purpose, and she will take care to have

them of bright colours, so as to make every process of her work
gay and pretty. A piece of coarse thread, double the length of
the lace required, is then folded in half, and pinned on the left
side of the cushion as it faces the worker. This double thread
is called the "foundation thread," and is pinned horizontally
across the cushion. A number of doubled threads—say half
a yard long when doubled—are cut ready and fastened on to the
foundation thread, as shown in Illustration 339.

Look at the illustration, and having pinned the foundation

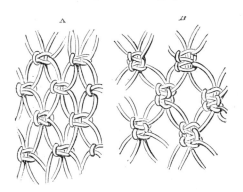

344.—Designs for Grounding, or Open Knotting.

thread as directed, take up one of the double lengths, and pass
the doubled centre downwards under the foundation thread, so
that the two ends are lying across the far side of the cushion;
then bring these two ends through the loop you passed under
the foundation thread, and draw up the stitch. The first row
of every pattern is worked in this way by putting on as many
threads as are wanted.

The next thing to be learnt is the Macramé knot, which
enters into every pattern, and is used in marking what is called
the cord—a pretty, close pattern, generally following close upon
the first row of the work.

The cord and Macramé knot illustrate each other, and are better learnt together. We suppose that the foundation thread is stretched upon the cushion, and the first row worked according to Illustration 339. Now consult Illustration 340.

You will notice that a second double foundation thread has been pinned on close to the stitches of the first row, and it is along this second thread that the cord is worked. The foun-

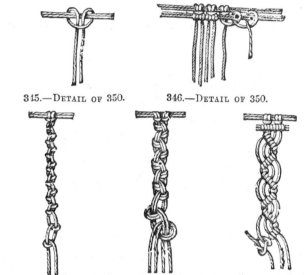

345.—Detail of 350.   346.—Detail of 350.

347.—Detail of 350.   348.—Detail of 351.   349.—Detail of 352.

dation thread is pinned at first only on the left side of the cushion, and must be held raised a little from the cushion in the right hand. Now take up in your left hand the first single vertical thread *, pass it over and then under the foundation thread and through the loop made by itself; draw up tight, and repeat from *. Proceed in the same manner with every thread in succession. Our illustration gives a useful hint to the learner by

showing the use of pins to hold the stitches well in place and
close together; and we may add that care should be taken not
to split the thread, but to stick the pins between two threads;
also to be careful to take the threads in their proper order.
Having worked the cord, there only needs a word as to the
Macramé knot. It is worked exactly as above described, the

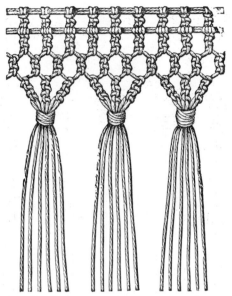

350.—FRINGE FOR ANTIMACASSARS, &c.

stitch being formed twice with the same vertical thread, as it is
the second half of the stitch which holds the first in place.

We come now to the Knotted Bar. This is a useful stitch,
and enters largely into all patterns. We again suppose the
cushion before you, with its cord neatly worked along the
second foundation row. Now consult Illustration 341.

You see that in the examples given four threads are used in

each bar. Beginning, then, with Fig. A, work with the two left-hand threads a single or half Macramé knot over the next two threads, and then work the same knot with those threads over the first two. Repeat this alternately, and you will have accomplished the double Macramé knot shown in Fig. A. It is called double because it is worked with two threads, not be-

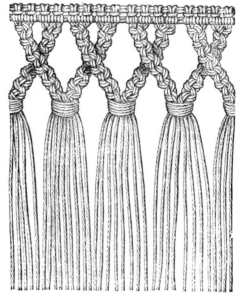

351.—FRINGE FOR ANTIMACASSARS, &c.

cause it is worked twice with the same threads. We give no further illustrations of this bar. Our fair pupil has already divined how it may be worked with single instead of double thread, with three over three, with half or complete Macramé knots, and so on. When she has exercised her skill in all these varieties she should turn to Fig. B, and work the buttonhole

knot. Again four threads are required; take three threads in
the left hand, in the right hand take up the fourth thread, pass
it over and then under the three threads, and draw it up, this
time not too tightly. The same remarks apply to this useful
knot as to the one represented in the preceding figure; varia-

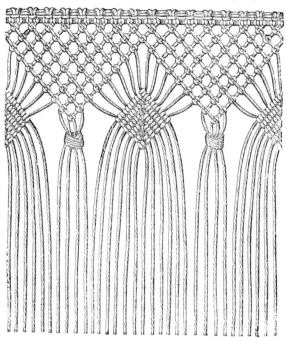

352.—Fringe for Antimacassars, &c.

tions of it will be easily recognised in patterns of Macramé
work, and will be copied without difficulty.

The next thing to be mastered is the Diamond or Star Pattern. We say " or " advisedly, for the one is but a variation of
the other. On looking at the best styles of Macramé lace, it

will be almost always found that this figure is worked imme-
diately beneath the cord described in Illustration 340. We give,
therefore, in the following diagram the usual heading of the
preceding illustrations. Now consult Illustration 342.

Sixteen single vertical threads must be set aside for this

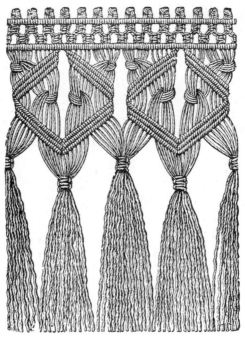

353.—FRINGE.

pattern; and for the present the eight right-hand threads had
better be twisted round a pin, and fastened on to the cushion,
out of the way. The pattern is now begun with the eight left-
hand threads, as follows:—Take the eighth, or right hand, thread
in your left hand, and hold it diagonally over the other seven

298

threads, letting it slope downwards at the angle shown in the
diagram.   This thread is technically known as the "leader:" it
is better to keep the term "foundation" threads for the horizontal ones.   Now take the seventh thread in your right hand,
and work over the leader a complete Macramé knot, keeping the

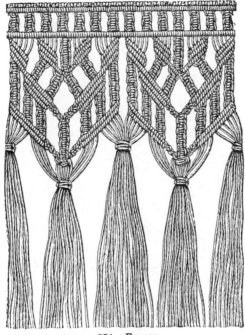

254.—FRINGE.

leader carefully in position. Repeat the Macramé knot with
every thread in succession down to the first, and pin the leader
to the cushion.   In some patterns only one leader is used, but,
as our diagram represents a double diamond, you will now take
the seventh or right-hand thread as a second leader; place it.

299

close to the first, and work over it with every thread in succession a Macramé knot, as before, of course, taking in the thread which formed the leader in the last row. Now unpin your

355.—MACRAMÉ FRINGE.

second group of eight threads. Take the first for the leader, and hold it diagonally across the other seven; take the second thread, and work a Macramé knot over the leader, do the same with every thread in succession, and pin down the leader as before. Then take the second thread for your leader, and work over it the second row of Macramé knots. By this time you will see that the upper half of your diamond is achieved. Use

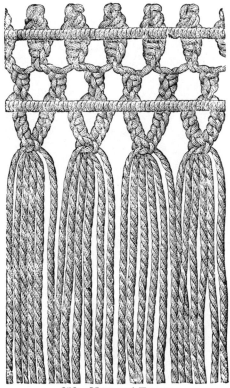

356.—Macramé Fringe.

pins freely in this part of the work, that your diamond may be true and firm. Now take the first left-hand thread as leader, slant it downward to the centre of the diamond over the other seven threads, and work your row of Macramé knots; then use the second thread as leader, working over it the second row. To finish the diamond, take the outer right-hand thread of the second group, and slant it down to the centre, work over it the row of Macramé knots; then take what is now the outer right-

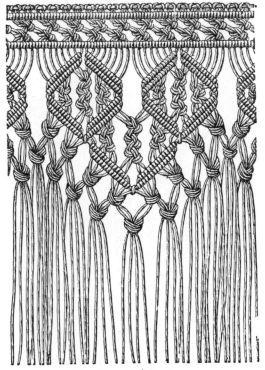

357.—MACRAMÉ FRINGE.

hand thread as leader, and work the second row. Lastly, tie the two centre threads together in a Macramé knot. By this time, we hope, the diamond is a complete success, and that our fair reader is already devising many an original combination to

302

vary the one just worked out as an example. As to the star, it is nothing but a diamond reversed—that is, it is begun with the first, or left hand, thread as a leader, and when half completed it is joined in the centre by tying two threads in a Macramé

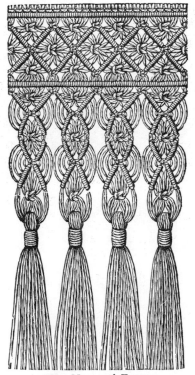

358.—MACRAMÉ FRINGE.

knot, as we directed in describing the diamond pattern. The three diagonal lines in Fig. B will often be claimed as old acquaintances in Macramé lace, although they may form no part of either star or diamond, and we hope that in whatever combination they occur they may present no difficulty. Very pretty centres are often worked in these diamonds with several of the ordinary lace stitches, and in our next diagram we give one of

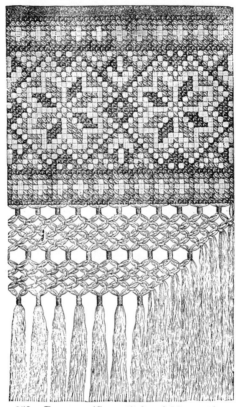

359.—FRINGE. (Cross-stitch and Macramé.)

the prettiest and most useful. It is generally known as the Italian or Genoese knot, but we advise our pupil to trust more to the diagrams and descriptions than to the names of the stitohos, for the latter vary considerably, and it may be that not

360.—MACRAMÉ FRINGE.

until she consults the diagram or pattern will she be reassured
that she is meeting with an old friend.

Now turn to Illustration 343, where you will recognise the half-completed star, with its centre Genoese knot. It is now supposed that the star has been joined together in the centre, and we begin our directions from that point. Take the four centre threads; we will number them from left to right, as 1, 2, 3, 4. Hold 1 tightly in the left hand, and with the right hand pass 4 over 3 and 2, under 1, over 1, under 2 and 3, and draw up

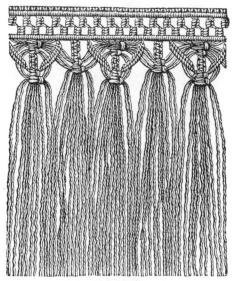

361.—MACRAMÉ FRINGE.

closely, but not too tightly; repeat eight times, so that you have a flat bar hanging vertically from the work. Now take a medium-sized bone or wooden knitting-pin, and lay it horizontally across this bar, take up all the four threads, pass them over the knitting-pin, above the knot which joined the star, thread them through the opening, bring them out again below the knitting-pin, and tie them tightly; then remove the

knitting-pin, and finish the star. The diagram shows in Fig. B
a knot called sometimes a Josephine and sometimes a Solomon's
knot. It is often used to form a heading, but when four Solomon's knots are tied in a diamond shape they make a pretty
centre to the larger diamond, shown in Illustration 342. For the
Solomon's knot proceed as follows:—Take the centre four
threads of a pattern, or four threads of a straight row, and

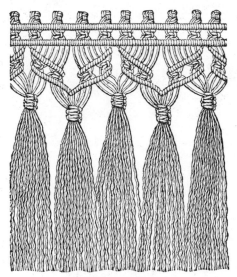

362.—MACRAMÉ FRINGE.

call them, as before, 1, 2, 3, 4. Hold 2 and 3 straight down
the cushion; bring 1 across them, so that it forms a loop,
then take 4 in your right hand, bring it downwards over the
end of 1 (which is lying horizontally across 2 and 3), pass it
under 2 and 3, and bring it upward through the loop between
1 and 2. Then take the threads one in each hand, and draw
them up close. This is one-third of the knot. Then, still keep-

ing 2 and 3 hanging straight down, take up 4, pass it across them

363.—Fringe for Parasols.

from right to left, so as to make a loop, take 1 and pass it downward over the end of 4 which is lying horizontally across 3 and 2, pass it under 2 and 3, and bring it up through the loop formed

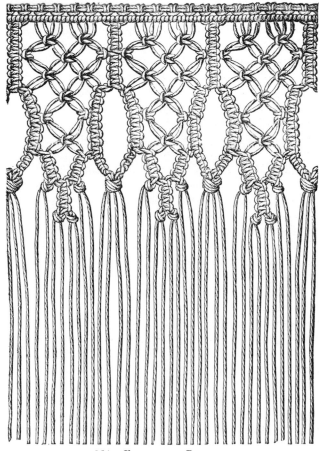

364.—Fringe for Parasols.

by 4, between 3 and 4. Take the two ends, and draw them up close. This is the second part of the knot. The third part is

nothing but a repetition of the first, and it must be remembered
that the complete Solomon's knot consists of these three parts.

In every stitch for which we have given directions so far the
thread has been always closely drawn up, and the lines sharply
horizontal or diagonal. Our next illustration shall give examples
of what is sometimes called open knotting, and it will be found
very useful to form a kind of network or filling up between the
more sharply defined parts of a pattern. It may spring from
almost any part of the work, and therefore it is represented in
the diagram without the usual indication of the cushion, or any
heading. Consult Illustration 344, and begin with Fig. A, as the
simpler pattern. The stitch is worked with four threads, from
left to right. Keep the two centre threads straight down, and
do not let them get crossed. Pass the first thread over the
second and third, and under the fourth; pass the fourth under
the third and second, and through the loop over the first, draw
up close, but not very tight; then, working from right to left,
pass the fourth thread over the third and second, and under the
first, then the first under the second and third, and through the
loop over the fourth, and draw up close, but not very tight.
This forms the knot. The next knot will not be made with the
same four threads, but the last two threads will be knotted to
the first two threads of the following knot, and so on. By this
time, with the aid of your pins, which are always useful in keeping
the work in place, and by consulting the intervals left in the
diagram for the circles and curves, the pattern will soon be reproduced upon the cushion, As to Fig. B, it is worked with
four threads in exactly the same way, only the knot is made
twice instead of once, as will be clearly seen on examining the
diagram. In treating of knotted bars, with the help of our
third diagram, we contented ourselves with explaining the two
there represented; but a very simple and effective bar is sometimes made by merely tying ordinary knots with two or four
threads, working alternately from right to left and left to right.

FRINGES.

For Antimacassars—Dresses—Mantles—Parasols—Cravats—Furniture, &c.

Nos. 345 to 352. Fringes for Antimacassars, &c. The materials selected for the fringes may be either thread, silk, wool, or fine cord. No. 350. Take a double thread of the length required for the fringe, fasten to the left and right side of the cushion, letting the loose end hang free. At intervals, along this double thread, a piece of thread folded in half is knotted as shown in Illustration 345. Each knotted thread is fastened to the cushion with a pin, and then the first row is worked with the double thread hanging towards the front of the cushion. Make a knot like a double buttonhole stitch, as shown in No. 347, holding quite straight and firm the thread round which the knot is made. 2nd row: Fasten a second horizontal line of double thread to the cushion, and, beginning at the left hand, make a double buttonhole stitch over it, as shown in Illustration 346. 3rd row: Like the first, only that 2 knots, instead of 1, are made. 4th row: Like the last, except that the knots are made between the 2nd of 1 double thread, and the 1st of the following one. 5th row: Like the last, but knotting 3 instead of 2 knots. In the 6th row 3 instead of 2 threads are knotted together, and the ends are cut off in regular lengths. No. 351. This fringe is begun like the preceding one, but in the 2nd row 6 double knots are made, as shown in Illustration 348. The rows of knots are then fastened together, as shown in illustration. No. 352 is begun in the same way, but the first row is knotted like the 2nd row of No. 350. 2nd row: Lay the 2nd end of the thread to be knotted over the 1st end, and make with the latter 2 buttonhole stitch knots. This kind of knot is made in the 9 following rows, and

a glance at the illustration will show which ends are to be
knotted together. The netted pattern having been framed, the
four strands of thread at the point of the vandyke are knotted
together, and the close pattern between the vandykes is knotted

355.—PARASOL.

as follows:—Take the 7th of the 12 threads, lay it across the
first 6 threads, and work from right to left, making 2 buttonhole stitch knots with each of the 6 threads; then place the 6th
thread over the 5 last of the 12, and proceed in the same manner
from left to right. (See Illustration 349.) Complete the close

pattern in the same way, using the 8th, 5th, 9th, and 4th threads, and so on, as the 7th and 6th were used.

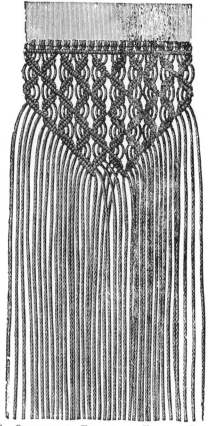

366.—ORNAMENTAL FRINGE FOR ENDS OF CRAVATS.

No. 353. Fringe. (Macramé Work.) Materials: White or écru-coloured thread. For illustration, fold in half 14 strands, each measuring 24 inches long, knot just where they are folded

313

in half, every 2 strands together (of course there are 4 single strands in the 2 doubled ones), knotting the 3rd and 4th over

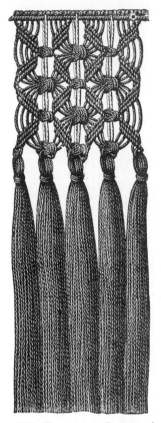 

367.—Fringe for Dresses, &c.   368.—Fringe for Dresses, &c.

the 1st and 2nd, and then the 1st and 2nd over the 3rd and 4th, 14 strands make one pattern. Having then begun as many patterns as you intend to knot, fasten the strands with a pin on

to a weighted cushion, and place a double horizontal thread
close under the knots. 1st row: Work from left to right as
follows:—2 buttonhole loops with every strand over the horizontal threads. 2nd row: 2 double knots with every 4 strands.
3rd row: The same, but in reversed position. 4th row: Like
the 1st row. 5th row: The intervals between the rows must be
copied from the illustration, and the strands are numbered as
they occur in each row. * Make a loose knot with the 5th to
the 8th strand, round the 1st to the 4th. † Place the 14th
strand aslant over the 13th to the 1st, and work 2 buttonhole
knots with each strand in order (13th to 1st) over the 14th;
repeat twice from †. Then knot the same pattern, but reversed
(see illustration), and repeat from *. 6th row: Like the preceding, but in the order shown in the illustration. 7th row:
Take the centre 14 strands of a pattern, and work a double knot
with the 1st and 14th strands over the 12 between, then do the
same with the last 7 of one pattern and the 1st of the next, and
cut the ends even.

No. 354. Fringe. Tie on to a double foundation thread a
number of folded strands, each 24 inches long and divisible by
14. 1st row: 2 buttonhole loops, with each strand in succession over a double foundation thread. 2nd row with 4 strands:
2 buttonhole loops, with the 4th over the 3rd and 2nd together,
2 buttonhole loops, with the 1st over the 2nd and 3rd, repeat.
3rd row: Like the 1st row. 4th row: * With 28 strands, 1
knotted row like the 2nd row, with the centre 4 of the 28
strands, but instead of the 4 double buttonhole loops 7 of
them, †; 1 leaf as follows: place the 1st strand aslant over the
2nd to the 6th, and work 2 buttonhole loops with each over the
1st, repeat twice from †, then a similar leaf, with the 7th to the
12th strand, with the 17th to the 22nd, and the 23rd to the
25th: these last must be knotted in reversed position. The last
knotted row of the two centre leaves are continued to the centre,
for which purpose two buttonhole loops are added with each of

the two first of the centre 4 strands over the foundation thread. The continuation of the pattern may be clearly seen from the illustration. The centre 16 strands of each pattern and the

309.—FRINGE FOR FURNITURE.

last 6 and first 6 of each pattern are then knotted together as in the fringe described in No. 353.

No. 355. Fringe. (Macramé Work.) Made with fine thread.

Take a number of strands of thread, about 12 inches long, and fold them in half, two at a time, then knot a loop with the 3rd and 4th strands over the 1st and 2nd, and then with the 1st

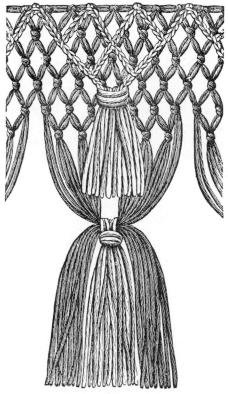

370.—FRINGE FOR FURNITURE.

and 2nd over the 3rd and 4th. Fasten each of the knots to the weighted cushion with a pin, and knot the 1st row as follows:— Place a double foundation thread horizontally across the ends

and close under the knots. Work from left to right, and knot
with each strand 6 buttonhole knots over the foundation thread.
Twelve strands make one pattern. 2nd row: 1 double knot with
every four strands. 3rd row: 2 double knots with the 3rd to
the 6th and with the 7th to the 10th, leaving the 1st and 2nd
and 11th and 12th unnoticed. 4th row: 1 double knot with the
5th to the 8th, leaving unnoticed the 1st to the 4th and the
9th to the 12th strands; then with every 12 strands work 1
double knot, using the four centre strands as a foundation
thread. To each knot add 4 new strands, folded in half, and tie
them round for a tassel, as shown in the illustration. Then add
4 new strands to those left unnoticed in the 4th row, and tie
them in the same way for a tassel. When the work is finished,
cut the strands even.

No. 356. Fringe for Dresses or Furniture. (Macramé Work.)
Material: Orient wool. Cut a number of lengths about 12
inches long, and folding them in the centre two at a time, make
a loop with the 3rd and 4th ends over the 1st and 2nd; and
then with the 1st and 2nd over the 3rd and 4th. Fasten each
knot so made on to the weighted cushion with a pin and then
knot the first row as follows;—Lay a double foundation thread of
wool horizontally across the ends and close under the row of
knots. Work from left to right 2 buttonhole knots with each
end over the double foundation thread. 2nd row: Take the 4th
thread and work 4 buttonhole knots over the 1st, 2nd, and 3rd
threads, repeat. 3rd row: Leave unnoticed the threads of the
first bar of buttonhole knots, * take the thread of the next bar
and knot with it 4 buttonhole loops over the previously used 3
foundation threads, repeat from *. 4th row: Like the 1st row.
5th row: * 4 buttonhole loops with the 1st end over the 2nd
and 3rd; then 4 buttonhole loops with the 6th over the 4th and
5th, repeat from *. 6th row: 1 double knot with the 1st and
6th strands over the 2nd to the 5th. Then cut the fringe even.

No. 357. Fringe. (Macramé Work.) Along a double foundation

318

thread knot strands of écru thread or purse silk, folded in half, and
measuring 28 inches. Illustration 357 shows how this is done.
Work from right to left. 1st row: Place a double thread across
the strands and work 2 buttonhole knots over it with each
strand in succession. 2nd row: 1 chain knot with the first 4
strands; this is done by knotting in buttonhole loop with the
first 2 over the second 2, and then with the second 2 over
the first 2. 3rd row: Like the preceding, but in reversed
positions, taking the 2 last ends of one set of 4 to work with
the first 2 of the next set of 4. 4th row: Like the 1st to
the 5th row. * Leave a space as the illustration shows, divide
into 16 strands, place the 8th strand slantwise over the first
7, and use it as a foundation thread; work 2 buttonhole stitches
in succession over it from the 7th to the 1st, and do the same
with the 10th to the 16th over the 9th; repeat from *. 6th
row: A close row of knots like the preceding. 7th row: With
the centre 4 of the 16 strands 3 chain knots as in the 2nd row,
then with the 4 strands on each side 1½ chain knots; repeat
from *. 8th and 9th rows: Like the 5th and 6th rows, but in
reversed position, and in the 9th row knot the centre 2 of the 16
strands so as to form a little square. 10th row: With the
centre 12 of the next 32 strands, 1 pattern as described in the
7th row. 11th and 12th rows: With centre 16 of 32 strands.
1 pattern like that of the 8th and 9th rows. 13th row: Knot
every 4 strands. 14th row: Like the 13th, but in reversed
position. The strands are then cut level.

358. Fringe. (Macramé Work.) Along a double foundation
thread, knot a number of strands of thread, folded in half and
measuring about 32 inches long. The number must be divisible
by 6. 1st row: With a double thread laid across the strands, 2
buttonhole stitches with each strand over the horizontal thread.
2nd row: 12 strands are required for one pattern, * 1 double
knot, with the 3rd to the 10th strand, using the centre 4 as a
foundation, and the outer ones to form the knots, 1 double knot

with the 11th and 12th, and 1st and 2nd of next pattern, repeat
from *.   3rd row: * Place the first of the 12 strands slantwise
over the 2nd to the 6th strands, and knot with each of the latter
2 buttonhole knots over the slanting strand, place the 12th
strand aslant over the 11th to the 7th, and knot as above, repeat
from *.   4th and 5th rows : Like the 2nd and 3rd, but with the

371.—Macramé Insertion.

pattern in reversed position. 6th row: Like the 2nd. 7th row :
Like the 1st. 8th and 9th rows : Like the 2nd and 3rd. 10th
row; 1 double knot, with centre 4 strands of each pattern,
leaving the other strands untouched. 11th row (see illustrations for distances): * Place the 6th strand aslant over the 5th
to the 1st, and work with each of the latter 2 buttonhole stitches
over the 6th, place the 7th over the 8th to the 12th strand, and

work over it as above, repeat from *. 12th row: * 1 tatted knot with the 2nd over the 1st, and with the 11th over the 12th. 1 double knot as before, with centre 8 strands. 13th row: Like the 3rd. 14th and 15th rows: Like the 11th and 12th, but without the tatted knots. 16th row (see illustrations for distances): 1 double knot, with each 12 strands, repeat, then

372.—Macramé Insertion.

thread 8 strands 4 inches long through the centre of each loop, tie them round to form a tassel, and cut the ends even.

No. 359. Border for Antimacassars. (Cross Stitch and Macramé Work.) This border, which is intended for any cover which has a straight edge, is worked in cross stitch, on yellow Russian lawn, with 2 shades of claret filoselle, and is then sewn on to a slip of claret plush or velvet. Every cross stitch takes in 4 threads of the lawn each way. Below the embroidery the lawn is unravelled, and every 16 threads are tied round with light and dark red silk alternately. Then follow in reversed position 4 rows of double knots. The 16 threads required for each double knot are then tied round again with red silk, and 4 more rows of double knots are worked as before. The tassels are then tied round, as shown in illustration, and the fringe is cut even.

No. 360. Fringe. (Macramé Work.) Materials: Silk, wool,

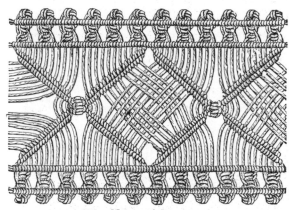

373.—MACRAMÉ INSERTION.

or thread. Along a double foundation thread of the required length knot a number of strands folded in half, and work from left to right. With 2 strands, 1 tatted knot with the right strand over the left. For the next row in reversed position 1 chain knot—that is, 1 buttonhole loop with the 1st strand over the 2nd, and then with the 2nd over the 1st—then change the ends, working the knot just described with the 2nd of the 1st double strand and the 1st of the strand following; then place a new strand over the knotted strands and tie one tatted knot over it with each strand in succession, then divide into patterns

24 strands each, and continue as shown in the illustration, working the bars in the chain stitch as above described. The principal figure in each pattern is worked with Josephine knots. For every figure of the close cluster of knots which surround the Josephine knots 3 strands are required. * Use 1 strand as a foundation, over which tie a buttonhole knot with the 2nd strand, and then a similar knot with the 3rd over the 2nd; repeat twice from *, but before beginning these knots tie a double knot round the strands of the chain stitch. The close

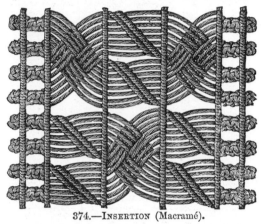

374.—Insertion (Macramé).

border which edges the vandyke of every pattern is tied like the knotted cluster above described; but the original foundation strand of 2 threads is strengthened after the point of the vandyke by the ends which have been left unnoticed as the pattern narrowed. The ends of the vandyke are then knotted together and cut even.

Nos. 361 and 362. Fringes. (Macramé Work.) No. 361. Along a double foundation thread knot a number of strands, 16 inches long and folded in half. 1st row: Place a double thread horizontally across the strands, and work over it 2 buttonhole loops

with each strand. 2nd row: 3 buttonhole loops, with the 4th
strand over the 1st, 2nd, and 3rd of every 4. 3rd row: 3 buttonhole loops, with the 4th strand over the first 3 of the next 4
strands. 4th row like the 1st. 5th row: Every pattern requires 24 strands. * With the 3rd to the 6th, and the 15th to the
18th, inclusive, 1 double knot over the 8 strands between; then
taking together the 7th and 8th, and the 13th and 14th, 1

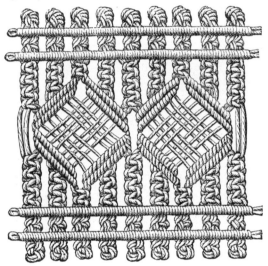

375.—Insertion (Macramé Work).

double knot over the 4 strands between; then with the 9th and
12th strands, 1 double knot over the 2 strands between; then 3
double knots with the 21st to the 24th strands; repeat from *.
6th row: * Twice place the 1st strand aslant over the 2nd to the
8th, and work over it 2 buttonhole loops with each; then twice
place the 20th strand aslant over the 19th to the 13th, and work
over it 2 buttonhole loops with each; repeat from *. 7th row:
* Take the 7th and 8th strands together, and the 13th and 14th

of tho noxt pattorn, and work 1 double knot over the 4 strands
between ; then take the 5th and 6th, and 15th and 16th, together,
and work 1 double knot over the 8 strands between ; then with
the 19th and 20th of this pattern, and the 1st and 2nd of the
next, 1 double knot over the 4 strands between ; then with the

376.—Insertion for Underlinen.

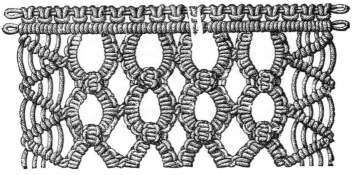

377.—Detail of Window-Drapery.

17th and 18th of this pattern, and the 3rd and 4th of the next
pattern, 1 double knot over the 8 strands between ; repeat from *.
Cut the ends even, and crimp them.—No. 362. The number of
strands must be divisible by 8, and measure about 16 inches
long. They are then folded in half, and every 2 are knotted

together in a buttonhole loop. This row of knots is then pinned
on to a weighted cushion, and the work begun. 1st row:
Place a double foundation thread across the strands, and, working from left to right, work 2 buttonhole loops with each over
the foundation thread. 2nd row: 1 double knot with every 4
strands. 3rd row: Like the 1st row. 4th row: Every pattern
requires 16 strands; the intervals must be copied from the
illustration, and the strands are numbered in the order in which
they are found when mentioned. * Place the 1st strand aslant
over the 2nd to the 8th, and work with the latter 2 buttonhole
loops in succession over the 1st; place the 16th aslant over the
15th to the 9th, and work with the latter 2 buttonhole loops in
succession over the 16th; repeat from *. 5th row: Like the 2nd
row. 6th row: Like the 4th row; but at the end of every
pattern work 2 buttonhole loops, with the 8th over the 9th
strand. 10th row: Turn back the first and last 4 strands of the
fringe on to the wrong side; fasten, and cut off the ends. * $2\frac{1}{2}$
double knots with the 5th and 12th of the next 16 strands over
the 6th to the 11th, take in the latter and use it as a foundation;
$2\frac{1}{2}$ double knots with the 13th strand of this and the 4th of the
next pattern over the 6 strands between; repeat from *. Cut
the ends even, and crimp them.

363 and 364. Fringes for Parasols, &c. These fringes may
be knotted with wool, thread, or silk. No. 363 requires a
foundation thread with strands 14 inches long, folded in half,
and fastened on at regular intervals. The 1st row is begun
from the left, two buttonhole loops being knotted with each end
over the doubled horizontal thread. 2nd row: 1 double knot
with the first 4 strands of thread. 3rd row: Like the first.
4th row: 20 strands are required for each pattern. * Take the
1st strand for a foundation thread, and, working from left to
right, make 2 buttonhole knots with each of the 2nd, 3rd, and
4th strands; then take the 8th strand as a foundation, and
working from right to left make 2 buttonhole loops with the 7th,

6th, and 5th strands respectively; then with the 9th and 10th and the 19th and 24th strands respectively make 3 double, followed by one single buttonhole loop; with the 11th and 12th and the 17th and 18th strand 2 double and 1 single buttonhole loop, with the 13th and 14th and the 15th and 16th strands 1 double and 1 single buttonhole loop; repeat from *. 5th row: * Cross the 14th and 15th strands and work from right to left, making with the 13th, 12th, 11th, 10th, and 9th ends in succession 2 buttonhole loops over the 15th strand; then from left to right make with the 16th, 17th, 18th, 19th, and 20th strands 2 double buttonhole loops over the 14th strand; then work with the 1st to the 8th strand in the same way as in the 4th row, consulting the illustration, taking in the 15th strand where the buttonhole loops end after the 1st buttonhole loop has been made with the 7th strand over the 8th; then, going back, take in the strands of thread, and then knot the 2 buttonhole loops with this 8th strand; repeat from *. At each repetition the 14th strand must be taken in with the 2nd strand of the next pattern. 6th row: * Take the 4th strand as a foundation and make 2 buttonhole loops with the 5th, 6th, 7th, and 8th strands respectively, then use the 5th end as a foundation, and make the loops with the 3rd, 2nd, and 1st strands; work in the same way with the 9th to the 20th strand as in the last row, *not* crossing the 14th and 15th strands, but always using as a foundation the strand nearest to the end where the knotting begins; repeat from *. 7th row: Like the last. The centre 2 of the 8 strands are not crossed, but knotted in the same way as the last 12 strands of this pattern; then follow 3 inserted rows as follows, which are knotted with the centre 6 of the last 12 of each pattern. In the 1st of these 3 rows the 3rd strand, in the 2nd the 2nd, and in the 3rd the 1st strand must be used as a foundation thread, and then making 2 buttonhole loops with the 4th, 5th, and 6th strands respectively; then repeat once the 4th to the 7th row, but in the reverse order, winding in the 1st row

the 7th strand round the 15th, and the 2nd round the 14th of
the previous pattern.   In the last of these 4 rows make 3 double

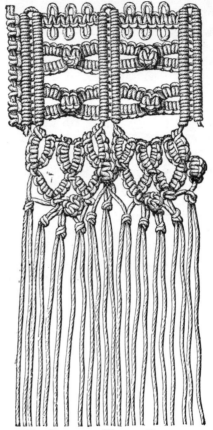

378.—Detail of Window-Drapery.

buttonhole loops with every 2 of the last 12 strands of each
pattern.   12th row : * The 1st strand of the next pattern but
one serves as foundation thread for the next pattern, making

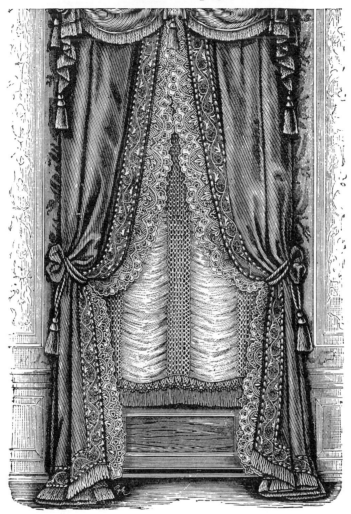

379.—WINDOW-DRAPERY.

over it 2 buttonhole loops with the 20th, 19th, 18th, 17th, and
16th strands respectively, with the 15th strand 4 buttonhole
loops over the same; then take the 8th strand as a foundation,
and make over it 2 buttonhole loops with the 9th, 10th, 11th,
12th, and 13th strands respectively, and with the 1st strand of
the following pattern, which has been previously used as a
foundation thread. 4 loops are then knotted with the 14th
strand, the other strands are left unnoticed; repeat from *.
13th row : Like the last. The 7th strand is used as the foundation for the first 6 strands, and the 2nd strand of the next
pattern but one is used as the foundation for the last 6 strands
of the next pattern. Instead of the 4 buttonhole loops worked
with the 14th and 15th strands, only 2 must be knotted, and
with the first end of the next pattern which formed the foundation thread of the last row work 2 buttonhole loops. 14th row :
Like the 2nd. Then knot together the 4 next ends as shown in
the illustration, and cut the ends even. 364. The first 2 rows
are knotted in the same way as in the last pattern. 2nd row :
* 4 double knots with the first 4 strands, close to the knots in
the last row. Twice (with the next 4 strands) 1 double knot ;
repeat from *. 3rd row : Leave the next 3 ends unnoticed, * 1
tatted knot with the following strand over the next 2 strands, 1
double knot with the next 4 strands, 1 tatted knot with the next
strand but 2 over the first 2 strands, leave the next 2 strands
unnoticed; repeat from *. 4th row : Like the 2nd row. 5th
row : Leave unnoticed the first 2 ends, * 3 double knots with
the following 4 strands, close to those of the previous row, 1
double knot with the next 4 strands, 3 double knots with the
next 4 strands close to those of the previous row ; repeat from *.
6th row : Leave the first 5 strands unnoticed, * 1 tatted knot
with the next strand over the next 2 strands, 1 tatted knot with
the next strand but one over the 8 previous ends, leave 6 ends
unnoticed; repeat from *. 7th row : Like the 5th, but 4
double knots must be made instead of 3. 8th row : Leave 2

strands unnoticed, * 3 tatted knots with the next strand over
the next strand. Twice (with the next 4 strands) 4 double
knots, 3 tatted knots with the next strand but one over the
previous strand; repeat from *. 9th row: * Knot the first 4
strands close to the knots of the previous row, knot the next 2
strands close to the other knots, 4 double knots with the next 2
strands, then knot every 2 strands together; repeat from *; cut
the ends even.

No. 365. Parasol. Parasol of écru batiste, lined with
white lutestring, and edged with the knotted fringe for which
we gave directions in the preceding paragraph. Cane stick
with silver chain and handle, in which is set a rock crystal.

No. 366. Ornamental Fringe for Ends of Cravats.
(Knotted Work.) For this pretty trimming the material
required is purse silk of the same colour as the cravat. Knot
together 20 ends of about 14 inches in length, folded in half and
placed within the hem of the cravat. These ends are fastened
with a few stitches and knotted across with a double foundation
thread, which is also fastened to the cravat, and passed horizontally across the 20 ends. 1st row : Take the threads in succession, and make with each two loops like a buttonhole stitch
over the foundation thread. Fasten the latter carefully at the
end of the row. 2nd row: 8 strands of thread form a pattern.
Take the first strand for a foundation thread, and make with the
next 3 strands 2 buttonhole loops each, over the foundation
thread from left to right; then, working from right to left, make
2 buttonhole loops with the 7th, 6th, and 5th strands over the
8th, used as a foundation thread. 3rd row: Like the second.
4th round : Take the 4th and 5th strand of a pattern ; use the
latter as a foundation thread, and make 2 buttonhole loops
across it, leaving the other strands unnoticed. Repeat 5 times
the 2nd to the 4th row, reversing the position of the design.
In the third repetition only the centre 32 strands, in the 4th
only the centre 24, and in the 5th only the centre 16 ends,

'leaving the others unnoticed. After the knotted work is over the ends are cut even.

Nos. 367 and 368. Fringes for Dresses, Paletots, &c. (Ma-

380.—TOWEL-HORSE AND TOWEL.

.cramé Work.) These patterns may be knotted with black or .coloured purse silk and fine gold thread. No. 367. Along a double foundation thread of black silk knot a sufficient number .of silk strands 16 inches long and folded in half. 1st row:

Towel Fringe.

Place a double thread horizontally across the strands and work over it 2 buttonhole knots with each strand in succession. 2nd

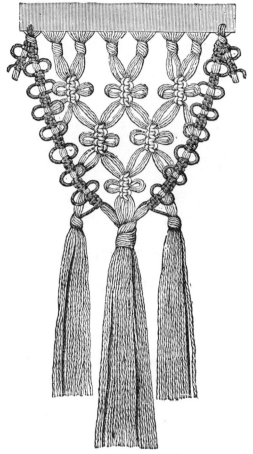

381.—DETAIL OF 380.

row: Each pattern requires 12 strands; * 3 times alternately place the 1st strand across the 2nd to the 6th (diagonally) and work over it 2 buttonhole knots with each in succession; then using the 12th strand as a leader, work a similar pattern in reversed position with the 7th to the 12th strands. Then thread through the knots of the 1st row a gold cord folded in half and measuring 4 inches long, so that it falls between the diagonal lines of each pattern. 3rd row : * 1 double knot over the gold cord with the 5th and 6th and 7th and 8th of the 12 strands ; then consult the illustration and repeat the 2nd and 3rd rows, letting

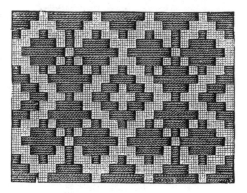

382.—DETAIL OF 380.

the pattern occur in reversed position. Then thread through every double knot of the last row a tassel of 10 strands each 6 inches long, tie them as shown in the illustration, taking in the gold cord; then wind them round with silk and cut the ends even. For No. 368 the strands must be about 24 inches long, and then the pattern is worked like the preceding to the end of the 1st row. 2nd row : Each pattern requires 12 strands * 1 buttonhole knot with the 4th to the 6th, over the 1st to the 3rd strands together, then 1 buttonhole knot with the latter over the former, then 1 buttonhole knot with the 4th to the 6th

334

over the 1st to the 3rd, then 9 buttonhole knots as above with the 7th to the 12th strands; repeat from *. 3rd row: 1 double knot with the 1st to the 3rd and the 10th to the 12th together. Repeat 8 times the 2nd and 3rd rows, letting the double knots occur in reversed position. The remaining strands are drawn together, and others added to form the tassels, which are then wound round as shown in the illustration, and the ends are cut even. Lastly a gold cord is threaded through the knots horizontally and vertically, and carefully fastened.

383.—Detail of 380.

Nos. 369 and 370. Fringes for Furniture, &c. No. 369. Tie along a foundation thread of the required length alternately 2 dark brown and 2 light brown strands of Orient wool folded in half, and work 2 rows of knots in reverse position with 2 threads for each knot. In the 3rd row knot together all the 4 strands of one shade. In the 4th row knot the 4th strand of 1 shade with the 1st of the other, and leave the intervening strands unnoticed. The remaining rows are knotted as is clearly shown in No. 369, but in the last row but 2 the 2 centre strands of each shade are knotted together, tied round with a few strands of the same

335

wool, and all the strands are then tied round with blue wool to form the tassels; then tie some blue wool to the foundation thread, * crochet 11 chain (at the interval shown in the illustration) to the foundation thread, and repeat from *. A tassel of brown and blue wool is then fastened on to each loop of chain, the upper part being sewn over with blue wool as shown in No. 369. For No. 370, tie along a foundation chain of the required length a number of strands of brown wool folded in half, and knot 4 rows in reversed position, then for every vandyke work 6 more knots, divide the strands as shown in the illustration, cross them and tie them with several shades of olive-green wool. For the vandyked border which lies along the upper part of the fringe, tie a strand of olive-green wool to the foundation thread; * (darkest shade) crochet 11 chain; join to the foundation thread and repeat from *. 3 of these loops must lie across 1 vandyke. Then finish each vandyke separately with pale olive wool as follows: join to centre stitch of 1st chain scallop: 5 chain: join to the last of the preceding row; fasten and cut the thread. Then join to each of the lower loops of chain a tassel made with several shades of olive-green wool, and cut the threads even.

INSERTIONS.

For Underlinen—Trimmings—Furniture.

Nos. 371 and 372. Insertions. (Macramé Work.) These two patterns look best when knotted with very fine thread. No. 371 is worked the long way, and is begun by tying double threads, of a yard long, to a double foundation thread. 1st row: Over a doubled horizontal thread, laid across the knotted strands, work 2 buttonhole-knots with every strand. 2nd row: 1 double knot with every 4 strands. 3rd row: Like the 1st row. 4th row: Measure the distances from the illustration, and remember that the strands are numbered according to their *apparent* order in the course of the work. For one diagonal pattern take 6 strands, 3 times alternately place the 6th strand aslant over the 5th, 4th, 3rd, 2nd, and 1st, and work over it 2 buttonhole loops with each of the latter in succession. 5th row: Like the 1st. 6th row: Like the 4th, but in reversed position. 7th to 9th rows: Like the 1st to the 3rd. 10th row: With 16 strands. To form the diamond, place twice alternately the 8th strand diagonally across the other 7, and with the latter work 2 buttonhole loops over the diagonal line; then work the same pattern in reversed position with the 9th to the 16th strands; then with the centre 12 strands, taking the first 3 and the last 3 together, and working with them 1 double knot over the other 6; then 2 patterns in reversed position, according to the illustration. The 4 knotted bars also take 16 strands, 4 to each bar; 6 times alternately 1 buttonhole knot with the 1st and 2nd end together over the 3rd and 4th together, and one buttonhole knot with the latter over the 1st and 2nd. When this row is finished, repeat 9 rows like the first 9, in reversed position. The projecting threads are then fastened on the wrong side and cut off. For No. 372, tie a number of strands to a doubled foundation thread; miss 2 strands, take the 3rd strand and tie it to the foundation thread *before*

384.—WINDOW-BLIND.

the preceding 2 strands, so as to form a loop (working from right to left), and work 14 buttonhole loops over it with the other end of the same thread; then work over the foundation thread 2 buttonhole loops with the 2 threads; repeat so as to form the row of loops shown in the illustration. 1st row: Over a double foundation thread, 2 buttonhole loops, with each strand in succession. 2nd row: 1 double knot with every 4 threads. 3rd

385.—DETAIL OF 384.

row: 4 buttonhole loops, with the 1st over the 2nd, and the 4th over the 3rd of every 4 strands. 4th row: 1 double knot, with the 3rd and 4th end of 1 pattern and the 1st and 2nd of the next. 5th to 7th row: Like the 3rd to the 1st, but in

reversed position. 8th row: With 28 strands place the 14th
strand diagonally across the 13th to the 1st, and work in succes-

386.—COLLAR (Macramé Work).

387.—WORK-BAG.

sion 2 buttonhole knots over it with each thread; then proceed in the same way, but in reversed position, with the 15th
strand placed across the 16th to the 28th; then 12 double

340

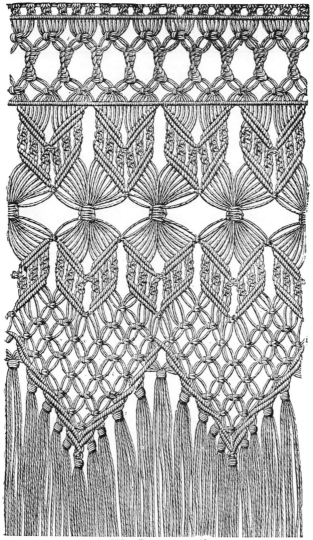

388.—DETAIL OF 387.

341

knots each with the 3rd to the 6th, the 7th to the 10th, the 11th to the 14th, the 15th to the 18th, the 19th to the 22nd, and the 23rd to the 26th. These knots are crossed, as shown in the illustration, and 1 double knot is worked with the 2 last strands of one and the two first of the following knot. Then work 2 diagonal lines as before, and the square is completed. The 8 rows which follow are like those at the beginning of the pattern; the projecting threads are then fastened down on the wrong side, and cut off.

No. 373. Various Purposes. (Macramé Work.) According to the use for which this is assigned, the insertion may be worked either in strong silk, thread, or tapestry wool. A number of strands, about 20 inches long, are folded in half, and knotted together once. Each of these knots is fastened with a pin to the weighted cushion, at the distance shown in No. 373. 1st row: Place a double foundation thread horizontally across the strands, and work over it 2 buttonhole knots with each strand in succession. 2nd row; (each pattern requires 4 threads) *, 2 buttonhole knots with the 4th of the first 4 strands over the centre 2, 2 buttonhole knots with the first strand over the centre 2, repeat from *. 3rd row : Like the first row. 4th row (each pattern requires 24 strands) : Twice alternately place the first of the 24 strands aslant over the 2nd to the 12th, and work over it 2 buttonhole knots with each strand in succession, then with the remaining 12 strands work a similar pattern, but in reverse position, using the 24th strand as a foundation thread. 5th row : * 1 raised spot as follows : $4\frac{1}{2}$ double knots, with the 23rd and 24th strands of 1 pattern, and the 1st and 2nd of the next, then thread the first of these 4 strands between the 23rd and 24th of the 4th strand, between the 1st and 2nd strands, from which the $4\frac{1}{2}$ double knots started, draw the strands tight, and work half a double knot, then, consulting the illustration, place the 9th, 10th, 11th, and 12th of the 24 strands over the 13th, 14th, 15th, and 16th, and under the 17th, 18th, 19th, and

20th, and place the 5th, 6th, 7th, and 8th strands under the 13th, 14th, 15th, and 16th, and over the 17th, 18th, 19th, and 20th strands, repeat from *. 6th row : Like the 4th, but the pattern must occur in reversed position. 7th to 9th rows : Like the 1st to the 3rd and 10th row, 1 buttonhole knot with the 3rd and 4th strands over the 1st and 2nd, repeat. Then turn back the ends, fasten carefully, and cut them close to the work.

No. 374. Insertion. (Macramé Work.) Our model is knotted with tapestry wool as follows : Fold in half a number of strands 16 inches long, and tie each in a double buttonhole knot, taking of course two doubled strands and making with the first two a buttonhole knot over the last two, and then vice versâ. These knots are then pinned on to a weighted cushion at the distances shown in No. 374, and a double foundation thread is laid across them. 1st row : 2 buttonhole knots with each strand in succession over the foundation. 2nd row : 2 double knots with every 4 strands. 3rd row : Like the 1st. 4th row : * Every 4 of the next 16 strands are put together to form one strand, pass the 3rd of these strands under the 2nd and over the 1st, the 4th over the 2nd and under the 1st, † twice alternately place the 8th end slantwise across the 7th to the 1st and work 2 buttonhole loops with each in succession over the first, then repeat once from †, and then from *. 5th to 8th rows : Like the 3rd and 4th alternately, but the pattern of the even numbered row must occur in reversed position. 9th and 10th rows : Like the 2nd and 1st. 11th row : 1 double buttonhole knot with every 4 strands. The ends are then turned back, and fastened down on the wrong side and cut off close.

No. 375. Insertion. (Macramé Work.) Fold in half a sufficient number of strands of unbleached thread about 16 inches long, taking care that the number is divisible by eight. Then tie together every 4 strands, making a loop with the 3rd and 4th over the 1st and 2nd, and with the 1st and 2nd over the 3rd and 4th. Each loop is then pinned on to a weighted cushion, and a double foundation thread is laid across the

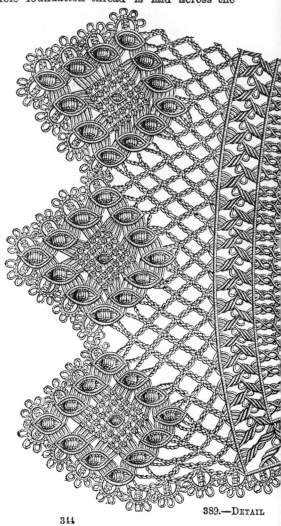

389.—Detail

strands. Then work from left to right as follows ;—1st row :

2 buttonhole loops over the foundation thread with every strand
in succession. 2nd row: 1 buttonhole loop with the 3rd and 4th
of every 4 strands over the 1st and 2nd, and 1 buttonhole loop
with the 1st and 2nd over the 3rd and 4th. 3rd row: Like the
1st row. 4th row: * 4 double knots with the 1st to the 4th
of the first 16 strands, 3 double knots with the 5th to the 8th,
2 double knots with the 9th to the 12th, and 3 double knots
with the 13th to the 16th, repeat from *. 5th row: Leave the
first two strands unnoticed, * twice alternately place the 8th of
the next 16 strands in a slanting direction across the 7th to the
1st strand, and make 2 buttonhole loops with each of the latter
in succession over the 8th strand, twice alternately place the 9th
strand in a slanting direction over the 10th to the 16th, and
work 2 similar loops with each over the 9th strand, repeat
from *. 6th row: Like the 5th, but in reversed position (see
illustration as to crossing the strands of each pattern). 7th to
10th rows: Like the 4th to the 1st, but in reversed order of
rows. 11th row: Like the 2nd row. Then turn back the 4
strands of every knot, and sew them firmly on the wrong side.
The projecting strands are cut away.

No. 376. Insertion for Underlinen. (Knotted Work.) Take
12 strands of thread two yards long and fold them in halves.
1st row: 4 tatted knots with the 1st over the 2nd, the 4th over
the 3rd, the 21st over the 22nd, and the 24th over the 23rd;
then 1 double knot with the first 4, the centre 4, and the last 4;
4 tatted knots with the 5th over the 6th, and the 20th over the
19th; 3 tatted knots with the 7th over the 8th, and the 18th
over the 17th; 1 tatted knot with the 9th over the 10th, and the
16th over the 15th. 2nd row: 2 buttonhole knots with the 11th,
10th, 9th, 8th, 7th, 6th, and 5th strand in succession over the
12th strand, and 2 buttonhole knots with the 14th to the 20th
over the 13th. Leave the first and last 4 unnoticed. 3rd to 8th
row: Like the preceding, using as foundation thread the strand
nearest to the beginning, and the strand used in one row is left

unnoticed in the following one, so that in the 8th row only 2 buttonhole loops are knotted. 9th row: 1 tatted knot with the 1st over the 2nd, and the 24th over the 23rd, 14 tatted knots with the 4th over the 3rd, and the 21st over the 22nd, 1 purl between the centre 2 of the 14; then 1 double knot with the first and last 4 close to the separate tatted knots, so as to form a loop with each, 2 buttonhole knots with the 6th to the 12th strand in succession over the 5th, and with the 19th to the 13th over the 20th, but before knotting this row draw the 5th and 20th strand through the purl of the loop. 10th row: 1 double knot with the 11th to the 14th strand, 7 times alternately 1 buttonhole knot with the 12th over the 11th, 1 with the 11th over the 12th, and 1 with the 13th over the 14th strand, then 1 double knot with the 4 centre strands, 15 tatted knots with the 9th over the 10th, and the 16th over the 15th strands, 1 purl between the 3rd and 4th, 6th and 7th, 9th and 10th, and 12th and 13th, 20 tatted knots with the 7th over the 8th, and the 18th over the 17th, joining the foundation thread to the nearest purl after the 4th knot (see illustration), and working 1 purl between the 6th and 7th, 10th and 11th, 14th and 15th knots, 25 tatted knots with the 5th over the 6th, and with the 20th over the 19th strand, joining to the purl after the 7th, 13th, and 19th tatted knots, and working 1 purl between the 9th and 10th, and 15th and 16th, * 7 tatted knots with the 1st over the 2nd, and with the 24th over the 23rd, 7 tatted knots with the 4th over the 3rd, and the 21st over the 22nd, joining to the purl after the 4th knot, 5 double knots with the first and last 4 strands. Repeat once more from *, pass the 4th and 21st strand through the nearest purls, and work 1 instead of 5 double knots with the first and last 4 strands. Repeat the 2nd to the 10th row as often as necessary.

VARIOUS HOUSEHOLD ARTICLES.

Window-Drapery—Towels—Window-Blind—Work-Bag—Basket for
Layette—Watch-Pocket.

Nos. 377 to 379. Window-Drapery. Long muslin curtains
under curtains of brown rep, which have a border embroidered

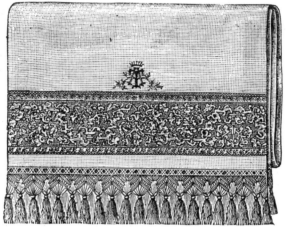

390.—Embroidered Towel.

on canvas in cross stitch. The design is worked with the following colours:—Etruscan red, yellow, pale blue, light red in wool
and filoselle. The rep curtains have also a fringe and tassels of
brown wool. White blind of fine holland slightly reeved, and
alternating with strips of open knotted work. The lower edge
of the blind has a border of the same work above a white fringe.
For the knotted work see Illustration 377. Along a double
foundation thread tie 34 strands of white cord about two yards

and a quarter in length. 1st row (from left to right). Along
a horizontal cord, 2 buttonhole loops with each strand. 2nd
row : Regulate the interval according to the illustration : 2 buttonhole loops with the 2nd, 3rd, 4th, and 5th strand successively
over the 1st strand, † 5 tatted knots with the next strand over
the 2 following, 5 tatted knots with the next strand but 3 over
the 2nd strand *before* it, joining as shown in the illustration ;.
repeat 3 times from †, then 2 buttonhole loops over the last.

391.—EMBROIDERED TOWEL.

strand with the 33rd, 32nd, 31st, and 30th strands successively.
3rd row : 2 buttonhole loops over the 5th strand with the 4th,.
3rd, 2nd, and 1st strands successively, † the next and the next
strand but 4 are left unnoticed, with the 4 strands between ;
proceed as follows :—Leave the 2 centre for the foundation and
knot 2 double knots over them with the 1st and 4th ; to form
the raised spot join the outside strand of the 4 to the beginning
of the knotted row, pulling through the ends with a crochet-
needle, and knotting 1 double knot close to it ; repeat 3 times

from †, then 2 buttonhole knots over the 30th strand with the
31st, 32nd, 33rd, and 34th strands successively; repeat the 2nd
and 3rd rows as often as necessary, and finish off with a row like

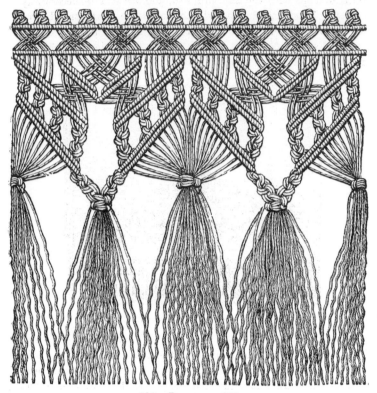

392.—Detail of 390.

the 1st. For the border and fringe see Illustration 379. Knot
8 strands about 2 yards in length to a cord which is passed in
the course of the work through the border, the latter being
worked the narrow way. The beginning of this cord must be on

the right side of the border.   1st row (from left to right): 2

393.—Detail of 391.

buttonhole loops over the cord with each of the 16 strands. 2nd

row (right to left) : Like the 1st row. 3rd row (left to right) :
† 5 tatted knots with the 1st strand over the 2nd and 3rd, then

394.—DETAIL OF 391.

with the next strand but 2, 3 tatted knots over the 2 preceding
strands ; repeat once more from † 7 double knots with the last 4
strands with 1 double purl between the 1st and 2nd, 3rd and

4th, and 5th and 6th.   4th row : † Leave **the 1st** and 6th strands untouched, 1 raised spot as before with the 4 centre strands ;

395.—DETAIL OF 391.

repeat once more from †.   The last 4 strands are left unnoticed. 5th row : † 3 tatted knots with the next strand over the 2nd next ones, 3 tatted knots with the next strand **but** 3, over the 2 preceding. The interval of the foundation cord which forms the scallop must be measured from the illustration; repeat from †. 6th row: Like the 1st row; repeat the 2nd to the 6th row as often as necessary, then join to every scallop of the border 6 strands of 16 inches in length. 1st row: 3 tatted knots with the 1st over the 2nd and 3 with the 4th over the 3rd; repeat. 2nd row: 1 double knot with every 4 strands. 3rd row: Leave the 2 first strands unnoticed, * twice alternately 3 tatted knots with the 1st over the 2nd and the 4th over the 3rd, then with the last 2 of one pattern and the first 2 of the next 1 raised spot; repeat from *. 4th row: 1 double knot with the first 4 of the centre 8 strands, the others left unnoticed. 5th row: 1 raised spot with the centre 4 strands of every pattern, then knot together every 2 strands; see illustration, and cut the fringe even.

Nos. 380 to 383. Towel-Horse and Towel. (Macramé Work). Stand of black polished wood. Towel of coarse cloth worked with red thread according to Illustration 383. Four threads of the ground are required for one stitch. The pattern must be carefully worked, and then the right and wrong sides will be exactly alike. The centre of the border has also a monogram in the same stitch. The pattern given in Illustration 382 may be used instead. The edges of the towel are fringed and knotted in the pattern shown in Illustration 380. Tie every 12 strands in a knot, and before tying the 1st, 7th, and 12th of every division, pass a double strand of blue thread through the work, then divide the 12 strands in half, 4 double knots with every 4 of the 12 white strands, forming purls as shown in the illustra-tion, 4 double knots with each 4 of the centre 8 strands, 4 double knots with the centre 4, then on each side of the pattern, using the white threads for the foundation, and taking in as required, the strands left unnoticed, 24 double knots with the blue threads on each side, consulting the illustration as to forming the purls and measuring the distances.

Window-Blind.

Nos. 384 and 385. Window-Blind. (Macramé.) This pattern, of which No. 385 gives a section in the original size, is begun as follows:—Cut a double foundation thread equal in length to the circumference of the frame and begin at the upper edge, which must measure one-fourth of the whole. Fold a number of strands, 2 yards long, in half, and tie them in the ordinary way to the foundation thread, taking care that the number is divisible by 12. Every pattern takes 24 strands, but the reverse rows begin and end with half a pattern worked with 12 strands. 1st row: Leave the 1st and last 12 strands unnoticed; then 1 double knot with the centre 4 of the next 24 strands; repeat all along the row, and then 1 buttonhole loop with the 1st of the first 12 and 12th of the last 12 over the foundation thread as follows:— Work 1 buttonhole loop from above downward, and then the 2nd from above upward over the foundation thread at the sides of the work. (See No. 385.) These buttonhole stitches are worked in every row. In the 2nd, 3rd, and 4th rows work 2, 3, and 4 double knots with the centre 8, 12, and 16 strands respectively; but in the 2nd row, 1 double knot with the first 4 of the 1st 12 and the last 4 of the last 12. In the 3rd row work the double knot with the 3rd to the 6th of the first 12, and the 7th to the 10th of the last 12. In the 4th row the double knots are worked with the 1st to the 4th and 5th to the 8th of the first 12, and with the 5th to the 8th and the 9th to the 12th of the last 12. 5th row: For one knotted pattern proceed as follows: 1 buttonhole loop with the last 4 strands of one pattern together over the first 4 of the next pattern; then with the latter over the former, 5 double knots with the centre 20 strands; repeat from *. Then 1 double knot with the 3rd to the 6th and the 7th to the 10th of the first and last 12 strands. 6th to the 8th rows: 1 double knot with every 4 strands; but the pattern must occur in reversed position. 9th row: Like the 5th, only that the knotted pattern is worked *after* the double knots. 10th and 11th rows: Like the 4th and 3rd. 12th row : 1 knotted pattern

355

like that of the 5th row with the last 8 strands of one pattern and the first of the next; then a similar knotted pattern with the last 4 of one pattern and the first 4 of the next: continue like the 2nd row. Now repeat as often as necessary the 1st to the 12th row. Then work another row like the first, and one in

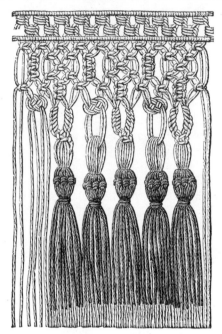

396.—Fringe for Towel.

which 2 buttonhole stitches are worked in succession over the foundation thread.

Nos. 386 and 389. Collar. (Macramé Work.) Worked with cream-coloured silk. Tie 159 strands, folded in half, and measuring 2 yards in length, to a double foundation thread about 10 inches long. After tying the strand to the foundation,

work close to the knot with 1 strand over the foundation
thread a buttonhole knot as follows :—1 buttonhole loop from
above downwards and from below upwards, working from
right to left. 1st row: 2 buttonhole knots with each strand
in succession over a double foundation thread placed close under
the first. 2nd row: The intervals must be measured according
to the illustration, and the strands numbered in the order in
which they occur. With 6 strands, 3 times alternately place
the 1st strand aslant over the 2nd to the 6th and work over
it 2 buttonhole knots with each strand. In the 3rd repetition
of this row work 4 buttonhole knots with the last thread over
the strand used as a foundation. 3rd row: Like the preceding,
but work the pattern in reversed position with the last 3 strands
of one figure and the first 3 of the next, copying the
beginning and ends of the rows as shown in No. 389, which gives
a section of the collar in the original size, adding new strands
as they are required to make the slanting line of the front of
the collar. 4th row: Like the 1st row. 5th row: * 4 buttonhole loops from below upward with the 1st of the 4 strands over
the 2nd, 4 buttonhole loops with the 4th over the 3rd, then 2
buttonhole loops with the 3rd over the 2nd, then 4 buttonhole
loops with the 4th over the 2nd, then 4 buttonhole loops with
the 2 corresponding strands, 2 buttonhole loops with the 2nd
over the 3rd strand; repeat from *. 6th to 8th rows: Like the
preceding, but in reversed position, and at the end of the 8th
row 2 knotted rows like the first 2 in the 5th row. 9th row:
Like the 1st row. 10th row: * 7 chain knots as follows (1
buttonhole loop with the 1st over the 2nd strand, and then with
the 2nd over the 1st) :—8 chain knots with the 3rd and 4th
strands, 9 chain knots with the 5th and 6th strands, 4 times
alternately place the 7th strand aslant over the 8th to the 12th
and work in succession 2 buttonhole loops over it with each
strand, then work a similar pattern in reverse position with the
13th to the 18th strands, then 9 chain knots with the 19th and

20th strands, 8 chain knots with the 21st and 28th strands, 7 chain knots with the 21st and 24th strands; repeat from *.
11th row: * Take 3 strands 1½ yards long folded in half, tie them to the 1st and 2nd of the next 6 strands so as to have 6 new strands there, then 4 double knots with the 1st and 6th strand over the 2nd to the 4th and the 6th new strands, then 5 chain knots with the 7th and 8th strands, 3 chain knots with the 9th and 10th, 1 raised spot as follows:—8 half double

397.—BAG FOR BATHING-DRESS.

knots with the 11th and 14th over the 12th and 13th strands, then take a crochet-needle and draw the strands which have just been used through the place where the 1st of the 8 double knots was tied, and knot the strands tightly close underneath the double knot so as to form the raised spot, 3 chain knots with the 15th and 16th strands, 5 chain knots with the 17th and 18th, then tie on 3 new strands with the 23rd and 24th as described above; repeat from *, but in every repetition except the last work the 4 double knots with the 19th strand of one pattern and the 6th of the next over the 10 strands between and

358

over the new ones. **12th row:** * 6 rows of chain knots with the
first 12 of the 36 strands as follows:—9, 8, 7, and then 3 times
6 chain knots, then 4 times alternately place the 18th strand
aslant over the 17th to the 13th, and work over it 2 buttonhole
loops in succession with each strand, then work the same pattern
in reversed position with the 19th to the 24th, then 6 rows of
chain knots like the former but in reverse order with the 25th

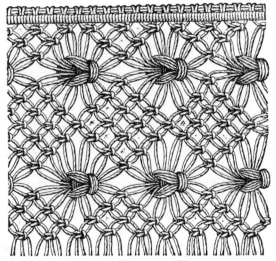

398.—Detail of 397.

to the 36th strand; repeat from *. **13th row:** Place the 13th
strand aslant across the 12th to the 1st and work over it 2
buttonhole loops with each strand, then 12 times place the
next of the first 12 (the 12th first) aslant over the 14th to the 17th
and work over it 2 buttonhole knots in succession with each
strand, then place the 18th strand over the 12 which were used
before as the foundation thread, and work over it 2 buttonhole
knots with each in succession, then work a similar pattern in

359

reversed position ; repeat from *. 14th row : * Twice alternately place the 6th strand over the 5th to the 1st and work over it 2 buttonhole knots with each in succession, then 1 raised spot as before with the 1st and 2nd strand over 2 new short strands tied on as a foundation, then twice alternately place the 1st strand over the 2nd to the 6th and work over it 2 buttonhole loops with each strand, then knot a similar pattern in reversed position with the 31st to the 36th, and work the raised spot with the last 2 strands of one pattern and the first 2 of the next, but not until the first knotted row of the 2nd pattern has been worked ; then consult the illustration, and by its help and that of the description already given work the centre pattern of the principal figure. The next 13 rows are like the first 13 but in reverse order; the rows of chain knots in the 16th to the 18th rows must be worked according to the illustration, and the last 4 rows must be continued to form the front of the collar, adding new strands as required by the shape. The 2 strands added to the lower edge of the border in the last row must be knotted just after the 6th strand has been tied ; they consist of 1 strand of a yard long folded in half, and are tied with 2 buttonhole loops over the foundation threads. 28th row : * 1 double knot with every 8 strands, using the centre 4 as a foundation, then 2 chain knots with the first 4, taking in 2 at a time, 2 chain knots with the last 4, taking in 2 at a time ; repeat from *. 29th and 30th rows : Like the preceding, but the pattern must occur in reversed position, and at the beginning of the 30th row, after having worked the double knot of the 3rd and 4th patterns, and then always after the double knot of the 5th and 6th patterns, 2 rows of chain knots 4 in each row, and 2 knots with every 2 strands. 31st row : * For a medallion pattern. With the centre 12 of 48 strands. Place the 24th strand over the 25th to the 30th and work over it 2 buttonhole loops with each strand, place the 25th over the 23rd to the 19th and work over it 2 buttonhole loops with each strand, the 24th over the 26th to the 30th and work over it 2 buttonhole loops with each strand, the 26th over the 23rd to the 19th and work over it 2 buttonhole loops with each strand, then with the 8 strands which have *not* been used as foundations 1 raised spot, then the last strand used as a foundation over the next 5, and work 2 buttonhole loops over it with each strand, then the corresponding strand is placed over the next 5, and 2 buttonhole loops worked with each strand, then a similar knotted row, and, lastly, a similar row with the corresponding strand on the other side, which completes the medallion. Continue the pattern of the 28th and 30th rows with the remaining strands, and repeat from *. The following rows, as may be seen from the illustration, are the same as the medallion patterns and the first rows of the border. The pattern inside the squares formed by the medallions is only rows of double knots in reversed position with a medallion in the centre. The row of purls round the border is worked as follows:—* 6 buttonhole knots with the first of 8 strands over the 2nd with 1 purl between the 2nd and 3rd and 4th and 5th. The purls are made by working the buttonhole stitch a little way off the preceding and then pushing it close up, then $2\frac{1}{2}$ double knots with the 3rd and 8th strand over the intervening ones, then these 6 strands placed by the one used before as a foundation and 6 buttonhole knots worked over them with 1 purl before the 1st and between the 2nd and 3rd and 4th and 5th; these knots must be tied very tight, so that the foundation does not seem too thick. Lastly, turn back the 8 strands on the wrong side of the work and cut off the projecting strands.

Nos. 387 and 388. Work-Bag (Macramé Work). Dark red plush bag, lined with silk of the same colour, hemmed and drawn up with a silk cord of the same colour. The macramé trimming is knotted from the pattern given in No. 388 with écru-coloured purse silk. Fold in half 162 strands of silk about 2 yards long and knot them to a double foundation thread tied in a circle. 1st round : 1 double knot with every 4 strands. 2nd round : A double foundation thread is laid across the strands, close under the knots, 2 buttonhole knots with every strand in succession over the foundation thread. 3rd round : 1 double knot with every 8 strands, using the centre 4 as a foundation. 4th round : 8 half double knots with the last 4 of one pattern and the first 4 of the next, using the centre 4 of these 8 strands as a foundation. 5th and 6th rounds : Like the 3rd and 2nd. 7th round : Every pattern requires 18 strands. * Twice alternately place the 1st strand across the 2nd to the 9th and work over it 2 buttonhole knots with each strand

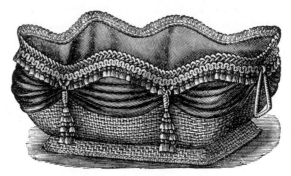

399.—Basket for Layette.

in succession, then work a similar pattern, but in reversed position, with the 10th to the 17th, then 1 double knot with the centre 4 of the 18 strands; repeat from *. 8th round : 1 double knot with every 3 strands, using only 1 strand as a foundation. 9th round : Like the 7th. 10th round : 3 double knots with the last 9 of 1 pattern and the first 9 of the next, using the centre 16 as a foundation. 11th to 13th rounds : Like the 7th to the 9th. 14th round : Every pattern requires 36 strands, and takes in the last 9 of the 1st pattern and the first 9 of the next but one ; * 1 double knot with the 7th, 8th,

Fringe for Layette.

9th, 10th, 11th, and 12th strands, and with the 25th, 26th, 27th, 28th, 29th, and 30th, using the centre 4 as a foundation, then

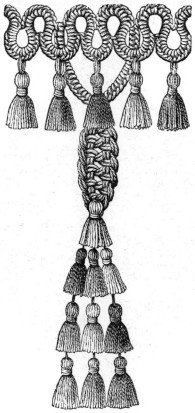

400.—DETAIL OF 399.

1 double knot with the 4th, 5th, 6th, 7th, 8th, and 9th, the 10th to the 15th, the 22nd to the 27th, and the 28th to the 33rd, using 2 strands as a foundation, then 6 times 1 double knot

363

with the next 6 of the same 36 strands, using 4 strands as a foundation : repeat from *. 15th round : * 5 separate double knots with the centre 30 of the 36 strands, using 2 strands as a foundation, then 4 separate double knots with the centre 24,

401.—WATCH-POCKET.

using 4 as a foundation, then 3 separate double knots with the centre 18, using 2 as a foundation, then 2 separate double knots with centre 12 strands, using 4 as a foundation, then 1 double knot with centre 6 strands, using 2 as a foundation; repeat from *. 16th round : For the outline of every vandyke * place the last 2 strands of one pattern over the first of the next, and work over them 2 buttonhole loops with each of the 6 in succession, then place the 3rd and 4th strand over the 5th and 6th, and work with the latter 2 buttonhole knots in succession, 2 buttonhole knots with the first foundation strands, and with the 7th to the 9th over 3rd and 4th, then place the 8th and 9th strands over the 10th to the 12th, and work 2 buttonhole knots

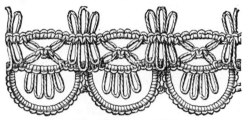

402.—Detail of 401.

403.—Detail of 401.

with them and with the former foundation strands, and with the next 3 strands over the 8th and 9th, and so on to the end of the vandyke. The other half of the outline is worked in the same pattern, but in reverse order, as shown in No. 388. 1 double knot is worked with the centre 6 strands at the end of each vandyke, using 4 strands as a foundation ; repeat from *.

Then knot the remaining strands to form the fringe as shown in the illustration, adding fresh strands when necessary.

Nos. 390 and 392. Towel. (Cross Stitch, Holbein and Knotted Stitch.) Towel of coarse white linen, with an embroidered border and knotted fringe at each end. When the pattern is worked, the towel is hemmed at each end, and the fringe is knotted with coarse white thread as follows. (No. 392.) A number of strands of about 24 inches long are folded in half, and knotted together two and two, by making a knot with the 2nd and 3rd strand over the 1st and 2nd, and then with the 1st and 2nd over the 2nd and 3rd. (See No. 392, which represents a pattern of the fringe in the original size.) The knots are then fastened to the weight cushion with pins in a straight line. Close underneath the knots arrange a double foundation thread, and work the 1st row from left to right as follows : 2 buttonhole knots, with each strand over the foundation thread. 2nd row : Like the preceding, but consulting the illustration, and tying together every 8 strands, by taking the 5th and 6th under the 4th and 3rd and over the 1st and 2nd, then the 7th and 8th over the 4th and 3rd and under the 1st and 2nd. 3rd row : Each pattern takes 32 strands, and the spaces must be measured from the illustrations, the strands being numbered according to the order in which they come in the work. * Knot the centre 8 of the 32 strands in the manner we described above, and then twice alternately carry the 9th end aslant across the 10th to the 16th, and work over it 2 buttonhole loops in succession with each strand, then work a similar pattern in reversed direction with the 17th to the 24th strands, then 2 buttonhole loops with the 16th over the 17th strand, plait the 9th to the 16th strands as above described, twice alternately carry one strand over the 2nd to the 16th, and work over it 2 buttonhole loops with each in succession, then work a similar pattern in reverse position with the 17th to the 32nd, repeat from *. 4th row : With every 4 strands, twice alternately 1 buttonhole loop with the 1st

366

and 2nd together, over the 3rd and 4th, and then with the latter over the former. 5th row: * Twice alternately carry the 1st end aslant over the 2nd to the 32nd, and tie with each in succession 2 buttonhole knots over it, then a similar pattern with the 17th to the 32nd, then with the 13th to the 16th, and the 17th to the 20th, work a row like the 4th row, but 3 instead of 4 double knots, then with the same 8 strands, 2 double knots with the 1st, 2nd, 7th, and 8th over the rest, but after the first double knot, take in 5 new strands, and tie them to the foundation thread and round the last double knot, then double knot with the last 12 of one pattern and the first 12 of the next, using the centre 8 as a foundation, then knot together the 1st, 2nd, 11th, and 12th on the wrong side, cut the strands even, and wind them lightly round a fine knitting-needle to make them curl.

Nos. 391, 393—396. Towel (Embroidery and Macramé Work). Coarse holland towel, embroidered with coloured cotton and white thread, and finished off at each end with knotted fringe. Trace the design upon the holland, and embroider the design as shown in Nos. 393 to 395 in chain, overcast, feather, knotted, and buttonhole stitch, filling up the figures in herring-bone, plain, and lace stitch. The outlines are worked with cotton, and the filling up put in with white thread. When the embroidery is finished, unravel about 4 inches of the holland at each end for the fringe, and knot it as follows :—1st row : Place a double foundation thread across the strands, and tie over it 2 buttonhole knots with each strand in succession. 2nd row : 3 buttonhole knots with every 4th strand over the preceding 3 strands. 3rd row : Like the 2nd row, but in reversed position. 4th row : Like the 1st row. 5th row : 1 double knot with every 4 strands. 6th row : Leave the first 2 strands unnoticed. * 4 double knots with the 1st to the 4th of the first 12 strands, 1 double knot with the 5th to the 8th, 1 double knot with the 9th to the 12th, 1 double knot with the 7th to the 10th, 1 double knot with the 5th to the 8th, 1 double knot with the 9th

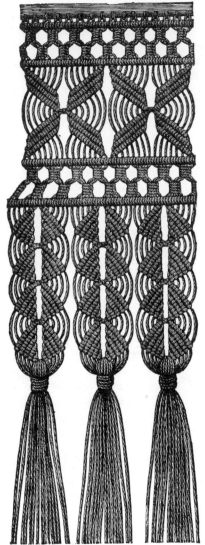

404.—DETAIL OF 405.

368

406.—TIE, WITH FRINGE.

to the 12th; repeat from *. 7th row: * 1 double knot with

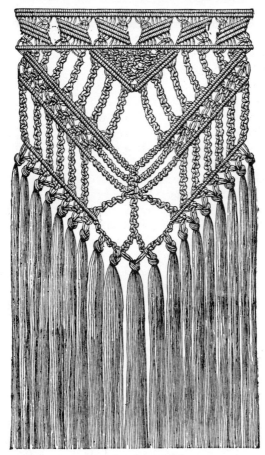

407.—DETAIL OF 406.

the 1st to the 4th strand, 1 double knot with the 5th to the 8th, 3 double knots with the 9th to the 12th; repeat from *

8th row : Leave the first 2 strands unnoticed. * 1 Josephine
knot with the 1st to the 4th of the first 12 strands, twist the
strands a short distance below (see No. 396), then thread 6
strands folded in half through the loop to form a tassel, add 5
double threads of blue cotton, tying them round in separate
knots, and then winding blue thread round all the strands
together and cutting the tassels even. Lastly, 6 buttonhole
knots with the 5th over the 6th to the 8th strands, and 6 with
the 12th over the 9th to the 11th strands ; tie the centre 2 of
these 8 strands, add 4 fresh strands as above, and tie $1\frac{1}{2}$ double
knot round them, and finish with a tassel like the one described
above.

Nos. 397 and 398. Bag for Bathing Dress (Knotting, Crochet,
and Netting). The bag itself is of brown leather, and is covered
with a pattern knotted in macramé work with fine string. The
sides are covered with netting, and so is the upper part, which
is drawn up with cord and tassels. The handles also have
large tassels on each side of the bag. For the macramé work
proceed as follows :—Along a foundation chain of the required
length knot a number of strands 2 yards long, folded in half,
and fasten the work to the weighted cushion. Over a double
thread placed horizontally across the strands (see No. 398) knot
the first row : 2 buttonhole loops with each strand in succession
over the horizontal thread. 2nd row (it takes 12 strands for a
pattern) : 1 double knot with the centre 4 of every 12 strands ;
these double knots consist of a right and a left knot as follows :—
Hold fast the centre 2 strands which serve as a foundation with
the third and fourth fingers of the left hand : for the left knot,
place the first strand loosely over the foundation threads towards
the right so that it makes a loop to the left, and hold it between
the thumb and forefinger of the left hand. Then pass the fourth
strand over the first and back again through the loop ; it must
go under the foundation threads, and upward through the loops.
Lastly, draw the knotted threads close together ; the right knot

is made in the same way, but in reversed order. 3rd row (for the space to be left consult No. 398): 1 double knot with the 3rd, 6th, and the 7th to 10th of every 12 strands. 4th row: 1 double knot with the 1st to 4th, the 5th to 8th, and the 9th to 12th of every 12 strands. 5th row: The first 2 and the last 2 strands are left unnoticed, 1 double knot with the 3rd and 4th strands of 1 double knot, and the 1st and 2nd of another; repeat. 6th to 8th row: Like the 4th to the 2nd row. 9th row: The first 6 and the last 6 remain unnoticed, 1 double knot with the last 6 of one pattern and the first 6 of the next, using the 4 centre strands as a foundation ; repeat the 2nd to the 9th row as often as necessary, but the last row of all must be like the 1st instead of the 9th, then cut off and fasten the projecting ends. The sides of the work form the upper end of the bag, and a horizontal thread is laid across them, over which a row of double crochet is worked which takes in the knotted strands at the same time. The macramé work and netting are then sewn on to the leather bag, as shown in No. 397.

Nos. 399 and 400. Basket for Layette (Macramé Work). Shallow, oblong basket of osier work, draped outside with blue cashmere, and edged round with macramé fringe and tassels. The cashmere is cut on the straight and must be 12 inches wide and the length required by the basket; it is then arranged in pleated scallops, as shown in Illustration 399. The macramé work round the upper edge is knotted with ivory silk as follows : Fasten on to a weighted cushion 4 strands of silk, each about 3 yards long; leave the 4th strand unnoticed, and * knot 12 buttonhole loops with the 1st strand over the 2nd and 3rd strands for a foundation ; then leave the 1st strand and knot 16 buttonhole loops with the 4th strand over the 3rd and 2nd; repeat from *. The smaller scallops form the upper edge of the border. Small tassels of ivory silk are tied to the lower scallops, as shown in Illustration 400. Also, according to the same illustration, join to ends folded in half to the 1st and 4th connecting cord, and for the left half of the scallop, knot 18 buttonhole loops with the 1st strand over the 2nd, 3rd, and 4th; and for the right half, 18 similar loops with the 4th over the 1st, 2nd, and 3rd. Then join the foundation threads, knot 1 double over the 6 foundation threads, using the 1st and 8th strand to work with. In the first 2 double, use only the centre 4 as foundation threads, and the 1st and 2nd and 7th and 8th to work with. Then * join the 8 strands, placing the 1st and 2nd in a loop under the 3rd to the 6th, then the 7th and 8th under the 1st and 2nd, and over the 5th and 6th; then again under the 1st and 2nd and over the 3rd and 4th, through the 1st loop; draw it up slightly and repeat 3 times from *. Then 3 double, as at the beginning of this pattern, and tie the ends

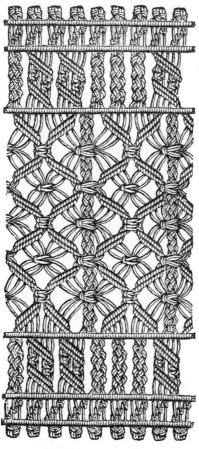

408.—Detail of 410.

together, adding tassels of different coloured silks, as shown in

Illustration 400. The layette is lined inside with blue cashmere.

409.—Detail of 411.

410.—Work-Bag.

411.—Side-Pocket.

Nos. 401 to 403. Watch-Pocket (Knotted Work). Pocket of claret-coloured satin with knotted work of écru-coloured thread. For the puffings of the front use claret-coloured satin, with rows of insertion in knotted work between each. The back of the pocket is of satin quilted in diamonds, and finished off with silk cord and small silk buttons. The wrong side of the pocket is cut out of cardboard, covered with claret-coloured silk. A metal ring crocheted round with claret-coloured purse silk is used to hang up the pocket, and the sewing on is hidden by loops of silk cord and tassels, arranged as shown in the illustration. For the knotted insertion (see Illustration 403) proceed as follows :—Along a double foundation thread knot 8 threads which have been folded in half, and so make 16 ends. 1st row : Pass the 8th end over the first 7, and use it for a foundation thread. Working from right to left, knot 2 button-hole loops with each thread. Then proceed in the same way from left to right with the 10th to the 16th end, using the 9th as the foundation. The strands of thread will always be numbered according to their position in the row which is being knotted. 2nd and 3rd row like the preceding one. Then follow 2 inserted rows. In the first of these 1 double knot is to be knotted out of the centre 4 strands of the 16, measuring the intervals according to the illustration. In the 2nd inserted row 1 double knot is knotted out of the centre 8 strands—that is, 1 double knot out of each 4 strands. 4th row : Use the 2nd strand as a foundation and work with the 1st strand * 2 tatted knots (these knots consist of a buttonhole loop from above to below, and a second buttonhole loop from below to above the foundation), 3 times alternately 1 purl, 1 tatted knot, then 1 tatted knot, then use the 15th end as a foundation, and repeat with the 15th from *, then 1 double knot with each 4 of the centre 12. Then follow 2 inserted rows as before, but in reverse order. 5th to 7th rows : Like the 1st to 3rd, but in reverse order (see illustration). 8th row : With the 1st strand over the 2nd and 3rd as foundation, and with the 16th over the 15th and 14th, 14 tatted knots each, with the 4th strand over the 5th and 6th, and with the 13th strand over the 12th and 11th,

9 tatted knots each, with the 7th strand over the 8th and with the 10th over the 9th 2 buttonhole loops each, then 2 double knots with the 2 centre 4 strands; twice alternately 1 double purl, 2 double knots, then with the 7th over the 8th strand, and with the 10th over the 9th 2 buttonhole loops each. Repeat the 1st to the 8th rows till the required length is knotted, fasten on new thread as often as required by means of a weaver's knot. For the lace (see Illustration 402) as follows :—Knotting the narrow way, knot 5 strands on to a double foundation, so that they make 10 strands. 1st row: 1 double knot with the first 4 strands on the left side, 1 double purl, 2 double knots as follows :—1 double knot with the 5th and 10th strands over the 6th, 7th, 8th, and 9th, then with the 9th over the 8th 20 tatted knots, inserting a purl between the 17th and 18th, which is joined to the scallop of the following row, 2 double knots with the 5th and 10th strands over the 6th and 7th. 2nd row: 5 tatted knots with the 1st strand over the 2nd, 5 tatted knots, 1 purl between each, with the 8th over the 7th strand, 2 double knots with the 3rd and 6th over the 4th and 5th strands at the interval shown by the illustration. 3rd row: 2 double knots with the 1st and 4th strands over the 2nd and 3rd, 3 double knots with a double purl between each, then 1 double knot, 2 double knots with the 5th and 8th over the 6th and 7th strands, 2 double knots with the 5th and 8th strands over the 6th, 7th, 8th, 9th, and 10th, 20 tatted knots with the 10th over the 9th strand, joining after the 3rd knot to the scallop in the previous row, and inserting 1 purl between the 17th and 18th knots, 2 double knots with the 5th and 8th over the 6th and 7th strands. Repeat the 2nd and 3rd rows till the required length is knotted.

ARTICLES OF DRESS, WORK-BAG,

ETC., ETC.

Cravats with Macramé Fringe—Work-Bag—Side-Pocket—Hanging
Work-Case.

Nos. 404 and 405. Cravat (Macramé Work). Navy blue
satin cravat, with a knotted fringe of navy blue purse silk. The
cravat should be 4 inches wide, and 32 doubled strands of silk
are knotted along each end. With these 64 strands proceed as
follows (from left to right) :—1st row ; Over a double thread
laid across the strands, 2 buttonhole loops with every strand in
succession. 2nd row : With every 4th strand, 4 buttonhole
loops over the 3 preceding strands. 3rd row : Like the preceding, but in reversed position. At the beginning and end of
this row work 4 buttonhole stitches with the 2nd over the 1st,
or the last over the last but one. 4th row : Like the 1st row.
5th row : The strands are numbered as they appear in the course
of the work. (See No. 404.) * (With 16 strands for 1 leaf
pattern) place the 1st strand slantwise across to the 8th and
work over it 2 buttonhole loops with each ; repeat from * ; and
then, with a similar pattern in reversed position with the 9th to
the 16th strand, using the 16th strand as the foundation, then
2 buttonhole stitches with the 8th strand over the 9th, then
another leaf pattern with the 1st to the 8th strand, in the same
position as that with the 9th to the 16th, and then another with
the 9th to the 16th strand like that with the 1st to the 8th.
6th to 9th row : Like the first 4, but in the 9th row, between
the 1st and 2nd strand and between the last and last but one,
knot with buttonhole loops 2 double strands, so that there are
8 single strands in the following row. 10th row : * (With 10
strands) for a triangular pattern, 5 times alternately pass the
6th strand over the 1st, and work over it 2 buttonhole loops

376

with each strand, decreasing in each row by 2 loops, and then a triangle in reversed position with the 7th over the 12th strand, then 2 buttonhole stitches with the 6th over the 7th; repeat 3 times from *, then take the 1st to the 6th and the 7th to the 12th strand, and tie them close to the last row. (See No. 404.) Pass 8 strands about 4 inches long above the loop between the knotted pattern, and tie them round like a tassel; repeat 5 knots from *. Cut the ends even.

Nos. 406 and 407. Cravat with Macramé Fringe. Blue silk ribbon scarf with a knotted white silk fringe, for which proceed as follows: Along a double foundation thread knot 30 strands folded in half. 1st row : Place a double thread across the strands, and work over it 2 buttonhole loops with each strand. The strands will be numbered as they appear in the course of the work. 2nd row (see Illustration 407) : 1 double knot with the 7th to the 10th strand, * place the 1st strand diagonally across the 10th and work over it 2 buttonhole loops with each strand; * repeat twice, then 1 double knot with the 1st to the 4th; repeat 5 times from *; the three last repetitions must be in reversed position. 3rd row; Like the 1st row. 4th row : 1 double knot with the first 4 of the centre 20 strands, then 4 double knots with the centre 16, 3 double knots with the centre 12, 2 with the centre 8, 1 with the centre 4, * place the 20th end across the 30th, and work over it 2 buttonhole knots with each; repeat once with the 19th strand from the last *, then the 41st and 42nd strands over the 40th to the 28th, and work 2 similar rows in reversed position. 5th row : Leave the first and last 2 strands unnoticed (see illustration), $6\frac{1}{2}$ chain knots with the 27th to the 30th, and with the 31st to the 34th, then 6 chain knots with the 23rd to the 26th, and the 35th to the 38th, then $5\frac{1}{2}$ chain knots with the 39th to the 42nd.

Nos. 408 and 410. Work-bag, of Plush. Bag of claret plush, drawn up with thin silk cord and tassels, and ornamented with knotted work of écru thread. Ruchings, bows and

ends of claret satin ribbon are then added, as shown in No. 410.
For the macramé work have ready a sufficient number of
strands, about one yard long, and folded in haif.   Make a loop
with the 3rd and 4th over the 2nd and 1st, and then a loop with
the 1st and 2nd over the 3rd and 4th.   Each knot so made is

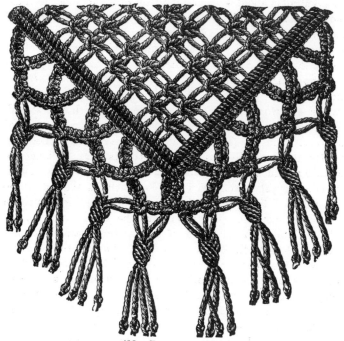

412.—DETAIL OF 411.

fastened with a pin on to the macramé cushion, so that they form
a straight line.   Then place a double foundation thread close
under the knots across the strand, and work from left to right.
1st row: 2 buttonhole loops, with each strand over the foundation thread.   2nd row: * With every 4 strands, 2 buttonhole

378

knots with the 3rd over the 4th, 2 buttonhole knots with the 2nd over the 3rd, 2 buttonhole knots with the 1st over the 2nd, repeat from *. 3rd row: Like the 1st row, but in this and the 5th row 3 more strands about 24 inches, folded in half, must be

413.—HANGING WORK-CASE WITH KNOTTED FRINGE.

taken; and in the course of the 4th, 6th, 7th, 8th, and 9th rows two such strands must be taken, and the requisite knots to be worked with them, as shown by the pattern, while in the 11th to the 15th rows the same number must be left out. 4th row: Every pattern requires 24 strands, the spaces must be measured

379

from the illustration, and the strands are numbered according to their apparent orders in the course of the work. * 5 times alternately with the 1st and 2nd strands together, 1 buttonhole knot over the 3rd and 4th, 1 buttonhole knot with the 3rd and 4th over the 1st and 2nd, then a row of knots like the preceding, with the 5th to the 8th and the 9th to the 12th, twice alternately place the 13th strand aslant over the 14th to the 18th, and work over it 2 buttonhole knots with each strand (14th to 18th) in succession; then with the 13th to the 15th and the 16th to the 18th half a knot each, using the centre strand as a foundation, then twice alternately place the 13th strand aslant over the 14th to the 18th, and work two buttonhole loops with each in succession over it; then work a similar pattern with the 19th to the 24th strands, and repeat from *. 5th row: Like the 1st. 6th row: (16 strands to a pattern) * twice alternately place the 6th strand aslant over the 5th to the 1st, and work over it 2 buttonhole loops, with each in succession; then knot a similar pattern in reversed position with the 11th to the 16th, twenty times alternating 1 buttonhole knot with the 7th and 8th over the 9th and 10th, and 1 knot with the 9th and 10th over the 7th and 8th, repeat from *. 7th row: 1 double knot with the 4th and 5th and 12th and 13th strands (taken respectively 2 together) over the 6th and 11th strands, and over the 7th to the 10th in the knotted row of this pattern; then using the 4 centre strands as a foundation, 2 double knots with the 14th to the 16th strands of this pattern, and the 1st to the 3rd of the next. 8th row: Twice alternately place the 1st strand aslant over the 2nd to the 6th, and work over it 2 buttonhole loops with each strand; then a similar figure with the 16th to, the 11th strand, but in reversed position. 9th row (see No. 408) : Like the 7th, but only one double knot instead of two. 10th to 13th rows: Like the 6th to the 9th. 14th to 16th rows: Like the 6th to the 8th. 17th to the 21st row: Like the 5th to the 1st. 22nd row: Take the 1st and 2nd strands together, and

work 1 buttonhole loop over the 3rd and 4th, and then do the
same with the 3rd and 4th over the 1st and 2nd.   Lastly :
Fasten the threads on the wrong side, and cut off the projecting
strands.

Nos. 409, 411, 412. Side-Pocket. (Knotted Work.) Pocket
of black grosgrain silk, 7 inches long in the longest part, and 5,
wide. A strong steel clasp closes the pocket, with tassels at
each end. The chain which suspends the pocket to the waistband is knotted in the pretty Josephine knot. The knotted
work is begun with the flap as follows :—Take a length of cord
measuring 6 inches for the foundation, and tie to it at intervals
lengths of 36 inches folded in half.   Then proceed as follows :—
1st row : Along a horizontal cord knot 2 buttonhole loops with
each end of cord.   2nd row : 1 double knot with 4 ends of
cords ; repeat 3rd and 4th rows : Like the 1st.   5th row : Leave
unnoticed the first 2 and the last 2 ends during the next 9 rows.
Divide the remaining ends into eights.   Form 1 double knot
with the centre four of each eight.   6th row : 1 double knot
with the first 2 and the last 2 of each eight, consulting the
illustration to see the length of cord which must be left between
the knots.   7th row : Like the 5th ; repeat 7 times the 5th to
the 7th rows, tatting knot with the 4th end over the 3rd.   In
the second 4 and the last 4 but one, only 4 tatted knots can be
formed instead of 5.   Then join these knotted fours at the
beginning and end with a double knot, and join on 2 ends at
the centre scallops at the point of the flap, join the 4 ends
together in a knot to form the fringe, and cut the ends even.
The pocket front is knotted in the same way, increasing the
number of ends as required by size of pattern.

Nos. 413 to 415. Hanging Work-Case with Knotted Fringe.
The pocket itself is cut out of blue grosgrain silk and batiste écru.
On the flap is a monogram between two broad straps of batiste
and knotted work edged with fringe. A metal ring crocheted
round with silk cord is attached to smaller similar rings on the

pocket by means of cord and tassels, and serves to hang it to the wall of the dressing-room or study. The cords and tassels are of blue silk, and the batiste on each side of the knotted work is arranged in puffings. For the knotted work, which is done the narrow way, see Illustration 415. Along a double foundation thread of écru twist join 12 threads folded in half,

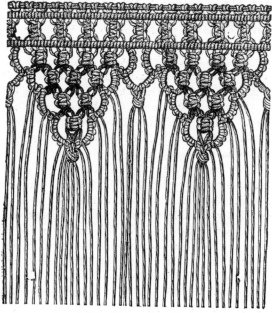

414.—DETAIL OF 413.

and measuring rather more than 2 yards. With these 24 strands work as follows the 1st row: Work from left to right over a double foundation thread 2 buttonhole loops with each strand one after the other. 2nd row: With the first 4 of the 24 strands 3 double knots; repeat. 3rd row: Like the 1st row. 4th row: With the 1st to the 4th strand and with the 21st to the 24th

strand 8 double knots, with the centre 16 strands 4 raised spots.
For each of these work 3 double knots with the next 4 strands
in succession, and then join to the 2 knotted strands where the
illustration shows. To do this draw the thread through with a
crochet hook and work 1 double knot on the right side of the
work. 5th row : With the centre 12 strands 3 raised spots as
before, with the 5th and 6th and the 19th and 20th 5 double
buttonhole knots each, then with the 1st over the 2nd, and the
24th over the 23rd end 1 buttonhole loop, with the 3rd to the
6th and with the 19th to the 22nd 1 double knot each. 6th
row : With the centre 8 strands 2 raised spots, with the 7th and

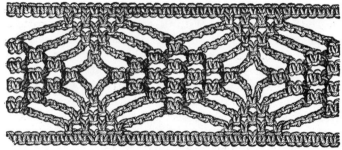

415.—DETAIL OF 413.

8th and with the 17th and 18th 4 double buttonhole loops each,
with the 1st to the 4th and with the 5th to the 8th, with the 17th
to the 20th and with the 21st to the 24th 1 double knot each.
7th row : With the centre 4 ends 1 raised spot, with the 9th
and 10th and with the 15th and 16th strands 3 double buttonhole knots each, with the 3rd to the 6th and with the 7th to the
10th strands, with the 15th to the 18th and the 19th to the
22nd strands 1 double knot each, with the 1st over the 2nd and
the 24th over the 23rd 1 buttonhole loop each. 8th row : With
the 11th and 12th and with the 13th and 14th strands 2 double
buttonhole knots each, then with all the 24 strands 1 double

383

knot with every 4, with the 11th and 12th and the 13th and 14th 2 double buttonhole knots each. 9th to the 11th rows: Like the 7th to the 5th rows, but in reverse order, then repeat the 4th to the 11th row as often as required, knotting 12 instead of 6 double knots in every repetition of the 4th row with the first and last 4 strands. The new pieces of thread are tied on in a weaver's knot. For the fringe see Illustration 414. It is worked the long way over a double foundation chain with folded strands of about 2 yards long. The first 3 rows are like the first 3 of the insertion, except that in the 2nd row 2 instead of 3 double knots are to be worked. 4th row: Every pattern requires 20 strands, 4 raised spots are knotted with the 16 centre strands, with the 1st over the 2nd and the 20th over the 19th 3 tatted knots each. With the centre 12 ends of a pattern 3 raised spots, with the 2nd over the 3rd and the 19th over the 18th 2 buttonhole knots each, then with the 3rd over the 4th and the 18th over the 17th 4 tatted knots, with the 2nd over the 1st and the 19th over the 20th $2\frac{1}{2}$ tatted knots, then with the 20th and the 1st strand of the following pattern 1 double buttonhole knot, after which knot together the 19th and 20th and the 1st and 2nd strands of the next pattern. 6th row: With the centre 8 strands of a pattern 2 raised knots, with the 4th and 5th and 17th and 18th 2 buttonhole knots, then with the 5th and 6th and 15th and 16th strands, 4 tatted knots. 7th row: With the centre 4 strands 1 raised spot, with the 6th and 7th and the 15th and 14th 2 buttonhole loops each, then with the 7th and 8th and 14th and 13th 4 tatted knots each, with the 8th and 7th and 13th and 12th 2 buttonhole loops each, and then the centre 4 ends in 1 knot. At the lower edge the strands are cut to an equal length, and the fringe is sewn on to the insertion with overcast stitches.